# CHINESE
# AMERICAN
# LITERATURE

GLOBE BOOK COMPANY

**Executive Editor:** Virginia Seeley
**Project Editor:** Kathleen Findorak
**Contributing Editor:** Beverly Ann Chin
**Art Director:** Nancy Sharkey
**Cover Design:** Richard Puder Design
**Interior Design:** Joan Jacobus
**Production Manager:** Winston Sukhnanand
**Desktop Specialist:** José López
**Marketing Manager:** Elmer Ildefonso

**Cover:** Untitled, by Pamela Chin Lee, *Asian American Arts Center*
**Photo Research:** Omni Photo Communications, Inc.

Literature, art, and photo acknowledgments can be found on page 154.

Printed in the United States of America.
1 2 3 4 5 6 7 8 9 10 96 95 94 93 92

**ISBN:** 0-835-90537-3

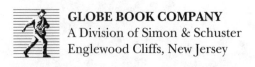
**GLOBE BOOK COMPANY**
A Division of Simon & Schuster
Englewood Cliffs, New Jersey

# CONTENTS

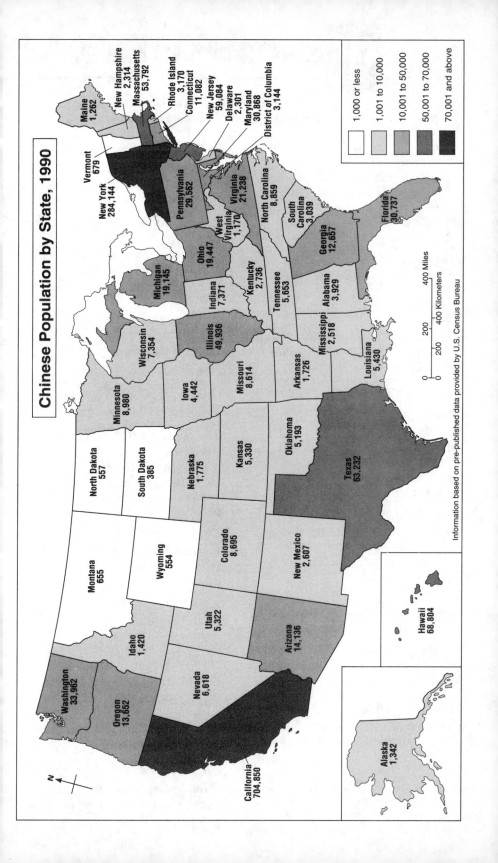

# Chinese Population by State, 1990

| | |
|---|---|
| | 1,000 or less |
| | 1,001 to 10,000 |
| | 10,001 to 50,000 |
| | 50,001 to 70,000 |
| | 70,001 and above |

New Hampshire
2,314

Maine
1,262

Massachusetts
53,792

Rhode Island
3,170

Connecticut
11,082

New Jersey
59,084

Delaware
2,301

Maryland
30,868

District of Columbia
3,144

Vermont
679

New York
284,144

Pennsylvania
29,562

West Virginia
1,170

Virginia
21,238

North Carolina
8,859

South Carolina
3,039

Florida
30,737

Georgia
12,657

Ohio
19,447

Michigan
19,145

Indiana
7,371

Kentucky
2,736

Tennessee
5,653

Alabama
3,929

Illinois
49,936

Wisconsin
7,354

Mississippi
2,518

Louisiana
5,430

Minnesota
8,980

Iowa
4,442

Missouri
8,614

Arkansas
1,726

North Dakota
557

South Dakota
385

Nebraska
1,775

Kansas
5,330

Oklahoma
5,193

Texas
63,232

Montana
655

Wyoming
554

Colorado
8,695

New Mexico
2,607

Washington
33,962

Idaho
1,420

Oregon
13,652

Nevada
6,618

Utah
5,322

Arizona
14,136

California
704,850

Hawaii
68,804

Alaska
1,342

400 Miles

400 Kilometers

0   200   400

0   200   400

Information based on pre-published data provided by U.S. Census Bureau

N

Titles of literature are placed in the time box to reflect, when possible, the historical time or event about which the selections are written.

*a chinese landscape painting in california—18?* ▼
**1849** California gold rush—Chinese population in United States rises dramatically.
**1860** 30,000 Chinese in California, 90 percent men

*Dragonwings* ▼
**1861–1869** Central Pacific Railroad is built.
**1870s–1900s** Increase in anti-Chinese violence
**1882** Passage of Chinese Exclusion Act bans Chinese immigration for 10 years.
**1895** Native Sons of the Golden State formed to help Chinese Americans advance in United States.

*Father Cures a Presidential Fever* ▼
**1910–1940** More than 175,000 Chinese immigrants processed on Angel Island in San Francisco Bay.
**1914–1918** World War I

*Lucky To Be Born A Chinese* ▼
**1924** Johnson-Reed Immigration Act imposes national quota system on immigration.

*Grandfather* ▼
**1929** Great Depression begins—12 to 25 percent of Chinese Americans unemployed

*Number One Son* ▼
**1937** Chinese Workers Mutual Aid Association is organized to gain better working conditions.
**1939–1945** World War II
**1949** People's Republic of China (PRC) is founded. Kuomintang moves to Taiwan.
**1950–1953** Korean War
**1952** McCarran-Walter Immigration and Nationality Act removes ban on Asian and African immigration to United States.

*Saying Yes* ▼
**1959** Hawaii elects first Chinese American Senator.

*A Soil With Rain And Sunshine* ▼
*Minority Poem* ▼
**Late 1960s–1970s** Dissatisfaction with continued discrimination in United States prompts forming of activist groups.

*The Struggle to Be an All-American Girl* ▼
*Lucky To Be Born A Chinese* ▼
*The All-American Slurp* ▼
**1965** Immigration Act of 1965 increases quota of Chinese immigrants from 105 to 20,000 per year.

*The Struggle to Be an All-American Girl* ▼
*My Mother's English* ▼
**1970s** Dramatic increase in college enrollment, of Chinese Americans, particularly women

*Chinatown #1* ▼
*Family Devotions* ▼
**1972** President Richard Nixon visits China.

*Lost Sister* ▼
**1978** California elects first Chinese American woman as secretary of state.
**1979** Vice Premier Deng Xiaoping of PRC visits United States.

*Eating Together* ▼
**1980** Chinese American men earn only 75 percent as much as white American men.

*Chinatown #1* ▼
*Family Devotions* ▼
**1989** Tiananmen Square massacre

# DEAR STUDENT,

All the cultures that make up the United States have played an important role in shaping the history of this country. In the following pages, you will read literature written by Chinese Americans. As you read the stories, speeches, plays, poems, and essays, reflect on the special customs and beliefs that are part of the Chinese American experience.

The literature is organized into four units. Each unit represents a special form of literature. The selections in the first unit are factual in nature and express the personal experiences of each writer. The second unit consists of fictional stories, the basis of which can be found in the cultural roots of the writers. The literature in the third unit presents two groups of poems. In the first group, the poets explore family relationships. In the second group, the poets reflect on their cultural identity. The fourth unit presents a drama that gives us a glimpse of the Chinese American experience as seen through the eyes of several generations.

The book also features a map that shows how the Chinese American population is spread throughout the United States. A time box provides information about historical events that occurred during the time period in which each selection is set.

As you read, think about the writing. The underlying themes represent the experiences of many who came to this country in search of the "American Dream." The writings of Chinese Americans not only reveal what makes their culture special but also highlight the commonality of all cultures.

# UNIT 1

# NONFICTION OF THE CHINESE AMERICANS

Unlike fiction, which deals with imaginary characters and events, **nonfiction** focuses on real life. The characters are real people, the settings are real places, and the events are ones that actually happened. Yet nonfiction is as creative and exciting as any other type of literature.

There are many forms of nonfiction, ranging from factual newspaper articles to very personal stories that unfold in autobiographies and biographies. Other forms of nonfiction include letters, diaries, journals, speeches, interviews, newspaper editorials, and essays. An important characteristic of all nonfiction is the inclusion of facts, or information that can be proved to be true. However, many writers of nonfiction combine facts with their personal thoughts, feelings, opinions, and values.

The personal aspect of nonfiction helps us to better understand different people, places, and times. The first selection in this unit is Elizabeth Wong's essay "The Struggle to Be an All-American Girl." This essay recounts Wong's childhood desire to abandon her Chinese heritage in favor of American customs and values. In "My Mother's English," Amy Tan explores the way in which her mother's "broken" English shaped her own perceptions about her mother, herself, and the world. Finally, the excerpt from Jade Snow Wong's autobiography, *Fifth Chinese Daughter*, conveys her appreciation for her cultural heritage by describing the rituals and customs of the Chinese New Year. As you read these selections, think about how the writers' most private thoughts and opinions are revealed through the way they describe factual events and situations.

Photograph of Chinese New Year celebration taken in San Francisco's Chinatown. Craig Aurness/Woodfin Camp and Associates.

*3*

# INTRODUCTION
## The Struggle to Be an All-American Girl

Born in 1958, Elizabeth Wong began her writing career as a journalist for the *Hartford Courant* and then the *San Diego Tribune*. Wong entered the Tisch School of the Arts at New York University with hopes of becoming a playwright. The following essay, "The Struggle to Be an All-American Girl," which she wrote as a young adult, first appeared in the *Los Angeles Times* in 1980.

When Wong was a young girl, her mother insisted that she learn the language and history of her Chinese heritage. In this essay, Wong vividly describes her childhood resistance to her mother's wishes and the embarrassment she felt about her background. Despite her protests, Wong and her brother were escorted by their mother to Chinese school each afternoon. Chinese school not only interfered with Wong's free time, but also clashed with her self-image as an "All-American" girl. As she recalls those days in the essay, she experiences a sense of loss and regret at having successfully rejected her cultural heritage.

# The Struggle to Be an All-American Girl

by Elizabeth Wong

It's still there, the Chinese school on Yale Street where my brother and I used to go. Despite the new coat of paint and the high wire fence, the school I knew 10 years ago remains remarkably stoically the same.

Every day at 5 P.M., instead of playing with our fourth- and fifth-grade friends or sneaking out to the empty lot to hunt ghosts and animal bones, my brother and I had to go to Chinese school. No amount of kicking, screaming or pleading could dissuade my mother, who was solidly determined to have us learn the language of our heritage.

Forcibly she walked us the seven long, hilly blocks from our home to school, depositing our defiant tearful faces before the stern principal. My only memory of him is that he swayed on his heels like a palm tree, and he always clasped his impatient twitching hands behind his back. I recognized him as a repressed maniacal child killer, and knew that if we ever saw his hands we'd be in big trouble.

We all sat in little chairs in an empty auditorium. The room smelled like Chinese medicine, an imported faraway mustiness. Like ancient mothballs or dusty closets. I hated that smell. I favored crisp new scents. Like the soft French perfume that my American teacher wore in public school.

There was a stage far to the right, flanked by an

American flag and the flag of the Nationalist Republic of China, which was also red, white and blue, but not as pretty.

Although the emphasis at the school was mainly language—speaking, reading, writing—the lessons always began with an exercise in politeness. With the entrance of the teacher, the best student would tap a bell and everyone would get up, kowtow[1] and chant, "*Sing san ho,*" the phonetic[2] for "How are you, teacher?"

Being 10 years old, I had better things to learn than ideographs[3] copied painstakingly in lines that ran right to left from the tip of a *moc but*, a real ink pen that had to be held in an awkward way if blotches were to be avoided. After all, I could do the multiplication tables, name the satellites of Mars and write reports on "Little Women" and "Black Beauty." Nancy Drew, my favorite book heroine, never spoke Chinese.

The language was a source of embarrassment. More times than not, I had tried to (dissociate) myself from the nagging loud voice that followed me wherever I wandered in the nearby American supermarket outside Chinatown. The voice belonged to my grandmother, a fragile woman in her 70s who could outshout the best of the street vendors. Her humor was raunchy, her Chinese rhythmless, patternless. It was quick, it was loud, it was unbeautiful. It was not like the quiet, lilting romance of French or the gentle refinement of the American South. Chinese sounded pedestrian. Public.

---

1. **kowtow** (KOW-tow) *v.* the act of kneeling and touching the ground with the forehead to show respect
2. **phonetic** (fuh-NET-ihk) *n.* speech sounds or the production of these
3. **ideographs** (IHD-ee-oh-grafs) *n.* graphic symbols representing an idea without expressing the sounds that form its name

In Chinatown, the comings and goings of hundreds of Chinese on their daily tasks sounded chaotic and frenzied. I did not want to be thought of as mad, as talking gibberish. When I spoke English, people nodded at me, smiled sweetly, said encouraging words. Even the people in my culture would cluck and say that I'd do well in life. "My, doesn't she move her lips fast," they'd say, meaning that I'd be able to keep up with the world outside Chinatown.

My brother was even more fanatical than I about speaking English. He was especially hard on my mother, criticizing her, often cruelly, for her pidgin speech—smatterings of Chinese scattered like chop suey in her conversation. "It's not 'What it is,' Mom," he'd say in exasperation. "It's 'What *is*, what *is*, what *is*!'" Sometimes, Mom might leave out an occasional "the" or "a," or perhaps a verb of being. He would stop her in mid-sentence. "Say it again, Mom. Say it right." When he tripped over his own tongue, he'd blame it on her: "See, Mom, it's all your fault. You set a bad example."

What infuriated my mother most was when my brother cornered her on her consonants, especially "r." My father had played a cruel joke on Mom by assigning her an American name that her tongue wouldn't allow her to say. No matter how hard she tried, "Ruth" always ended up "Luth" or "Roof."

After two years of writing with a *moc but* and reciting words with multiples of meanings, I finally was granted a cultural divorce. I was permitted to stop Chinese school.

I thought of myself as multicultural. I preferred tacos to egg rolls; I enjoyed Cinco de Mayo more than Chinese New Year.

At last, I was one of you; I wasn't one of them.

Sadly, I still am.

# AFTER YOU READ

## Exchanging Backgrounds and Cultures

1. How does Wong's description of the Chinese school reveal her childhood attitude toward her cultural heritage? How is this attitude reflected in the way she views her grandmother?
2. What does this essay suggest about Wong's childhood perceptions about being an American?
3. What does the last sentence of the essay reveal about the way Wong's attitude changed as she matured?

## What Do You Think?

Which character, image, or event in this essay is especially meaningful to you? Why did it stand out?

## Experiencing Nonfiction

In her essay, Wong offers some insights into the community where she grew up. What are your feelings about your own community? How would you describe it to someone who has never been there? Write an essay in which you convey your impressions of your community.

**Optional Activity** Write a description of your school. Think about how you want others to "experience" your school. One way to create a vivid description is to use images, or words that appeal to one or more of the five senses.

# *INTRODUCTION*
## My Mother's English

The daughter of Chinese immigrants, Amy Tan was born in Oakland, California, in 1952. At the time, tensions between Chinese Americans and their white neighbors were easing. But tensions between generations of Chinese American families were growing. This was especially true of the relationship between Chinese-born women and their American-born daughters.

In an attempt to become more Americanized these daughters often rejected the traditionally obedient role of Chinese women. Although their mothers struggled to preserve their heritage, they also strongly encouraged their daughters to pursue ambitious professional careers.

These conflicts defined the relationship between Amy Tan and her mother. Tan resisted her mother's plans for her to become a neurosurgeon and concert pianist. Tan wanted so badly to become "American" that she considered plastic surgery to change her appearance. It was not until her first visit to China, at age 35, that Tan accepted her Chinese heritage and started to think of herself as both Chinese and American. In the following speech, "My Mother's English," Tan discusses the ways in which her mother's English, a distinct combination of Chinese speech patterns and English words, influenced her perceptions of her mother, herself, and the world around her.

# My Mother's English

by Amy Tan

As you know, I am a writer and by that definition I am someone who has always loved language. I think that is first and foremost with almost every writer I know. I'm fascinated by language in daily life. I spend a great deal of time thinking about the power of language—the way it can evoke an emotion, a visual image, a complex idea, or a simple truth. As a writer, language is the tool of my trade and I use them all, all the Englishes I grew up with.

A few months back, I was made keenly aware of the Englishes I do use. I was giving a talk to a large group of people, the same talk I had given many times before and also with notes. And the nature of the talk was about my writing, my life, and my book *The Joy Luck Club*. The talk was going along well enough until I remembered one major difference that made the whole thing seem wrong. My mother was in the room, and it was perhaps the first time she had heard me give a lengthy speech, using a kind of English I had never used with her. I was saying things like "the intersection of memory and imagination," and "there is an aspect of my fiction that relates to this and thus." A speech filled with carefully wrought grammatical sentences, burdened to me it seemed with nominalized forms, past perfect tenses, conditional phrases, all the forms of standard English that I had learned in school and through books, a form of English I did not use at home or with my mother.

Shortly after that I was walking down the street with my mother and my husband and I became self-conscious of the English I was using, the English that I do use with her. We were talking about the price of new and used furniture and I heard myself saying to her, "Not waste money that way." My husband was with me as well, and he didn't notice any switch in my English. And then I realized why: because over the twenty years that we've been together he's often used that English with me and I've used that with him. It is sort of the English that is our language of intimacy, the English that relates to family talk, the English that I grew up with.

I'd like to give you some idea what my family talk sounds like and I'll do that by quoting what my mother said during a recent conversation which I video-taped and then transcribed.[1] During this conversation, my mother was talking about a political gangster and who had the same last name as her family, Du, and how the gangster in his early years wanted to be adopted by her family which was by comparison very rich. Later the gangster became more rich, more powerful than my mother's family and one day showed up at my mother's wedding to pay his respects. And here's what she said about that, in part, "Du Yu Sung having business like food stand, like off the street kind; he's Du like Du Zong but not Tsung-ming Island people. The local people call him Du, from the river east side. He belong that side, local people. That man want to ask Du Zong father take him in become like own family. Du Zong father look down on him but don't take seriously until that man become big like, become a Mafia. Now important person, very hard inviting him. Chinese way: come only to show respect, don't stay for dinner. Respect for making big celebration; he shows up. Means gives

---

1. **transcribed** (tran-SKREYEBD) *v.* to write or type out in full

lots of respect, Chinese custom. Chinese social life that way—
if too important, won't have to stay too long. He come to my
wedding; I didn't see it I heard it. I gone to boy's side. They
have YMCA dinner; Chinese age I was nineteen."

You should know that my mother's expressive command
of English belies how much she actually understands. She
reads the *Forbes Report*, listens to *Wall Street Week*, converses
daily with her stock-broker, reads all of Shirley MacLaine's
books with ease, all kinds of things I can't begin to
understand. Yet some of my friends tell me that they
understand 50% of what my mother says. Some say maybe
they understand maybe 80%. Some say they understand
almost nothing at all. As a case in point, a television station
recently interviewed my mother and I didn't see this program
when it was first aired, but my mother did. She was telling me
what happened. She said that everything she said, which was
in English, was subtitled in English, as if she had been
speaking in pure Chinese. She was understandably puzzled
and upset. Recently a friend gave me that tape and I saw that
same interview and I watched. And sure enough—subtitles—
and I was puzzled because listening to that tape it seemed to
me that my mother's English sounded perfectly clear and
perfectly natural. Of course, I realize that my mother's English
is what I grew up with. It is literally my mother tongue, not
Chinese, not standard English, but my mother's English which
I later found out is almost a direct translation of Chinese.

Her language as I hear it is vivid and direct, full of
observation and imagery. That was the language that
helped shape the way that I saw things, expressed things,
made sense of the world. Lately I've been giving more
thought to the kind of English that my mother speaks. Like
others I have described it to people as broken or fractured
English, but I wince when I say that. It has always bothered
me that I can think of no other way to describe it than
broken, as if it were damaged or needed to be fixed, that it
lacked a certain wholeness or soundness to it. I've heard
other terms used, "Limited English" for example. But they

seem just as bad, as if everything is limited, including people's perceptions of the Limited English speaker.

I know this for a fact, because when I was growing up my mother's limited English limited my perception of her. I was ashamed of her English. I believed that her English reflected the quality of what she had to say. That is, because she expressed it imperfectly, her thoughts were imperfect as well. And I had plenty of empirical[2] evidence to support me: The fact that people in department stores, at banks, at supermarkets, at restaurants did not take her as seriously, did not give her good service, pretended not to understand her, or even acted as if they did not hear her.

My mother has long realized the limitations of her English as well. When I was fifteen she used to have me call people on the phone to pretend I was she. In this guise, I was forced to ask for information or oftentimes to complain and yell at people that had been rude to her. One time it was a call to her stock broker in New York. She had cashed out her small portfolio and it just so happened that we were going to New York the next week, our very first trip outside of California. I had to get on the phone and say in my adolescent voice, which was not very convincing, "This is Mrs. Tan." And my mother was in the back whispering loudly, "Why don't he send me check already? Two weeks late. So mad he lie to me, losing me money." Then I said in perfect English, "Yes I'm getting rather concerned. You had agreed to send the check two weeks ago, but it hasn't arrived." And she began to talk more loudly, "What you want—I come to New York, tell him front of his boss you cheating me?" And I was trying to calm her down, making her be quiet, while telling this stock broker, "I can't tolerate any more excuses. If I don't receive the check immediately I'm going to have to speak to your manager when I arrive in New York." And sure enough the following week, there we were in front of this astonished stock broker. And there I was, red-

---

2. **empirical** (ihm-PIHR-ih-kuhl) *adj.* based on experiment and observation

faced and quiet, and my mother the real Mrs. Tan was shouting at his boss in her impeccable broken English.

We used a similar routine a few months ago for a situation that was actually far less humorous. My mother had gone to the hospital for an appointment to find out about a benign brain tumor a CAT scan had revealed a month ago. And she had spoken very good English she said—her best English, no mistakes. Still she said the hospital had not apologized when they said they had lost the CAT scan and she had come for nothing. She said that they did not seem to have any sympathy when she told them she was anxious to know exact diagnosis since her husband and son both died of brain tumors. She said they would not give her any more information until the next time; she would have to make another appointment for that, so she said she would not leave until the doctor called her daughter. She wouldn't budge, and when the doctor finally called her daughter, me, who spoke in perfect English, lo-and-behold, we had assurances the CAT scan would be found, they promised a conference call on Monday, and apologies were given for any suffering my mother had gone through for a most regrettable mistake. By the way, apart from the distress of that episode, my mother is fine.

But it has continued to disturb me how much my mother's English still limits people's perceptions of her. I think my mother's English almost had an effect on limiting my possibilities as well. Sociologists and linguists will probably tell you that a person's developing language skills are more influenced by peers. But I do think the language spoken by the family, especially immigrant families, which are more insular, plays a large role in shaping the language of the child. . . . [While this may be true, I always wanted, however,] to capture what language ability tests can never reveal—her intent, her passion, her imagery, the rhythms of her speech, and the nature of her thoughts. Apart from what any critic had to say about my writing, I knew I had succeeded where it counted when my mother finished reading my first book and gave me her verdict. "So easy to read."

# AFTER YOU READ

## Exchanging Backgrounds and Cultures

1. What does this speech reveal about Tan's earlier attitude toward her mother? How has this attitude changed over time?

2. How has Mrs. Tan's English shaped the way in which her daughter approaches her writing?

3. How does Mrs. Tan's difficulty communicating in English affect the way she is treated by others? What does this suggest about the way immigrants are viewed by mainstream society?

## What Do You Think?

Which part of this speech did you find most interesting? Why was it meaningful to you?

## Experiencing Nonfiction

Tan uses lessons she learned from her mother as the main point of her speech. Write an essay in which you convey a lesson you learned from someone else. Use this lesson as the main point of your essay. Support your main point with details and examples.

*Optional Activity* Think of an experience you had involving communicating with others. Write a speech or personal account about the outcome of that experience. Be sure to bring the experience to life by using dialogue and vivid description.

## *INTRODUCTION*
### Lucky To Be
### Born A Chinese

The following excerpt is from Jade Snow Wong's autobiography, *Fifth Chinese Daughter*. Written when Wong was 27, the autobiography captures the experiences of a young Chinese American girl caught in the confusion of growing up in a traditional Chinese home while attending American schools. As the fifth daughter of a rigid and strict father, Wong was expected to adhere to certain Chinese customs and values, such as respect for and obedience to one's elders and responsibility for younger brothers and sisters. These values often conflicted with the strange ways of her American classmates. As Wong struggles to find her own identity, she remains loyal to the traditional ways of her parents and celebrates the rituals of the community in which she was raised.

The excerpt you are about to read, "Lucky To Be Born A Chinese," captures Wong's devotion to her family and her cultural heritage. Using vivid imagery and ample detail, Wong describes the traditional beliefs and rituals associated with the joyous holiday of the Chinese New Year.

# Lucky To Be Born A Chinese
## from *Fifth Chinese Daughter*

by Jade Snow Wong

THE MONTHS FILLED WITH SCHOOLWORK, MUSIC LESSONS, AND home chores were broken in routine by a few days which glowed. These were the seven days of the Chinese New Year. According to the Chinese lunar calendar, New Year's fell in the American February, unless it was a Chinese "leap year," which gave the year an extra seventh month. These holidays climaxed the year and the American-Chinese children at public school were excused for their festivities.

. . . The Wong children, all scrubbed and with their hair washed, were dressed in new clothes, for New Year's literally meant that everything should be new, renewed, or clean. The children also tried to be very good, for a scolding on New Year's day foretokened frequent scoldings during the year. It was also poor taste to talk about unpleasant subjects, such as death, for that would also bring bad luck; therefore visitors uttered the most flattering remarks and offered exaggerated good wishes, such as, "May you be blessed with a hundred sons and a thousand grandsons!" or "May you enjoy the best of health and longevity!"[1] or "May you find your great material fortune this year!"

---

1. **longevity** (lahng-JEV-uh-tee) *n.* long life

The sidewalks on both sides of Grant Avenue were lined with colorful exhibits when "The New Year's Thirtieth Night" or New Year's Eve approached. Huge branches from blossoming trees, such as the peach, pear, or apricot, were placed beside open-tiered shelves laden with pots of flowering azaleas, camellias, gardenias, cyclamen,[2] and early-budding bulbs of narcissus[3] and daffodils. Because of its delicacy and heavenly fragrance the traditional narcissus bulb with double blossoms, which grew in water, was always the favorite. . . .

Mama took Jade Snow and Jade Precious Stone and Forgiveness from Heaven through the streets to see all the sights, for although Mama would not leave the house the year 'round, on "The Year's Thirtieth Night" it was her privilege and desire to go out and enjoy the community gaiety for one evening.

The streets, narrow to begin with, were now made even narrower by the displays; they were also jammed by shoppers looking for choice purchases. The busy hum of the crowd and the merchants' cries created an undercurrent of excitement. A festive spirit flowed from the well-dressed children and their dressed-up mothers, all seemingly relaxed and carefree in their holiday mood and costumes.

Mama did not buy anything; she had her hands occupied with Forgiveness and Jade Precious Stone. Besides, Daddy had already bought all their groceries for their wonderful New Year's meals—one feast tonight for "Rounding Out the Year" and one day after tomorrow to "Open the Year."

On New Year's Eve, when they got home, they discovered that Daddy had gone out too by himself and had brought back a huge branch of pink blossoms, which now graced their one and only antique vase, a handsome black porcelain piece

---

2. **cyclamen** (SEYE-kluh-muhn) *n.* a plant in the primrose family, having heart-shaped leaves and white, pink, or red flowers
3. **narcissus** (nahr-SIHS-uhs) *n.* bulb plant with smooth leaves and white, yellow, or orange flowers

with a colorful dragon decoration. The faint perfume of almond blossoms pervaded their dining room. . . .

The Wongs expected callers every day of the New Year week, and they were prepared not only with a spotless home but also with decorations of bright oranges and tangerines neatly stacked on plates, new potted plants, and red hangings and pillow covers.

Jade Snow helped Mama pass sweetmeats and red melon seeds to their guests. The sweetmeats were candied melon, coconut, or kumquats,[4] and lichee nuts[5] from China. The red melon seeds were consumed by the visitors with remarkable skill. They cracked the tiny kernel's outer shell with their teeth, and extracted the thin white seed expertly without breaking it, continuing this tirelessly all afternoon without interrupting their conversation. (In a Chinese gathering melon seeds took the place of cigarettes; and during visits, at the theater, and at banquets, the click, click, click of cracking shells always told of a sociable occasion.) The red and green colors, the fruit, the green plants, the flowering branches, the seeds, the sweets—all were propitious: they meant life, new life, a fruitful life, and a sweet life.

During New Year's, Chinese women worked at jobs irregularly or not at all; the most important thing was to celebrate properly. The women who were regularly employees of Daddy's visited his home as guests. There were many exchanges of sweets, and Jade Snow was never hungry during that week. In addition, callers tucked into the children's hands at least a quarter and sometimes fifty cents or a silver dollar, wrapped in red paper for a good-luck token of material wealth during the year. Mama reciprocated by giving the callers' children similar good-

4. **kumquats** (KUM-kwahts) *n.* orange-colored, oval fruit the size of a plum, with a sour pulp and a sweet rind
5. **lichee nuts** (LEE-chee NUTS) *n.* single seeds surrounded by sweet edible pulp, enclosed in brown, papery shells

luck packets. Some of Jade Snow's schoolmates returned to class with tales of the amount of gift money they had kept for themselves, but she always had to give hers back to Mama.

The delicious tidbits exchanged at New Year's varied according to the pride and custom of individual households. Some prided themselves on steamed sweet puddings, made of brown sugar and special flours, and decorated with red dates or sesame seeds. Others specialized in salty puddings, made with ground-root flour (something like potato flour), fat pork, chopped baby shrimps, mushrooms, red ginger, and green-topped with parsley (baby coriander leaves). Some families brought a special deep-fried dumpling filled with ground soybeans and rolled in sesame seeds, to be eaten piping hot. Still other women spent considerable time in making tiny turnovers which consisted of a delectable filling of chopped roast pork, bamboo shoots, and spices, rolled in a thin, chewy, translucent paste, and steamed on bamboo racks. . . .

At the Wongs', the New Year week got a good start at the "Opening of the Year" with an extra-bountiful dinner which featured Daddy's special chicken dish and a huge roast duck. The celebration also had a good wind-up on its seventh and last day called "The Day Man Was Made," with another feast. Of course, the dinner did not end with chicken or duck; there were special dried-vegetable-and-oyster stews and other time-consuming dishes which were not usually served.

To "Open the Year," Daddy—who cooked only when he was enormously pleased with the occasion—usually fixed his lichee chicken. . . .

During the week that followed, there were Lion Dances daily on the streets. Daddy took them to watch the dancing, now holding Forgiveness high on his shoulder, to watch the performance from unobstructed heights. It was the custom in San Francisco for the Chinese hospital to raise its yearly funds by engaging a "lion" to dance for his money. A group of acrobats trained in the technique relieved one another in these dances. They used a large and ferocious-looking but very colorful "lion's head," fitted with bright eyes on springs, and a jaw on hinges. From this head there hung a fancy satin "body" and "tail" piece, sewn together with different-colored scalloped strips of coral, turquoise, red, green, and blue silk. One man who set the tempo for the dance manipulated the head, holding it up in both hands, with only his brightly trousered and slippered legs showing below. As the huge Chinese drums beat in quickening tempo, he danced hard, raised the head high, and jerked it from side to side in an inquiring and delighted manner. His partner, holding up the tail, danced in accompaniment. Their lively movements simulated the stalking, attack, and retreat of a lion.

Citizens of Chinatown co-operated by hanging red paper tied with currency and lettuce leaves in front of their doorways. The lion approached and danced up to the prize. Sometimes, he had to dance onto a stool to reach it. As he stretched his hand out through the mouth to grab the money, his feet keeping time on the stool all the while, the occupant of the house or store threw out strings of bursting firecrackers, both to welcome him and to scare away the evil spirits. Daddy, with Jade Snow, Jade Precious Stone, and Forgiveness from Heaven, followed the lion's trail, treading the red fragments of burnt firecracker wrappings which carpeted the gray sidewalks.

Jade Snow was always fascinated by the Lion Dance—the insistent strong beat of the drums was exhilarating, and the colors and rhythm were unforgettable. But sometimes she felt sorry for the lion, especially when it was hot, or when the bursting firecrackers were thrown right at the "fearless" animal.

The firecrackers were set off to frighten away any lingering evil spirits, and to make the New Year fresh and clean. They came from China and were of various sizes. The tiny ones were hardly worth burning, and were useful to pack with stored clothing to keep away moths. The next size was most popular. In a continuous string they made a great deal of noise, and singly they were still effective. . . . There were still bigger ones which Jade Snow was not allowed to burn. These were called "big lights" and could blow up a bottle or lift a tin can. . . .

Another festival which was traditional with the Chinese and therefore with the Wong family was the Moon Festival.

As long as Jade Snow could remember, their family had unfailingly and appropriately observed the holiday, which was said to have originated in ancient China. According to the Chinese lunar calendar, on the fifteenth day of the eighth month the moon would rise rounder, larger, and more brightly golden than at any other month of the year. Then, specially baked cakes filled with a thick, sweet filling were eaten by the Chinese in recognition of the beautiful, full harvest moon. The round Chinatown moon cakes which Jade Snow knew were about four inches in diameter and an inch and a half thick. Thin, short, sweet golden pastry was wrapped around rich fillings of ground lotus pods,[6] or candied coconut and melon, or ground sweetened soybean paste. Jade Snow's favorite filling was "five seeds." This was a crunchy, sweet, nutty mixture of lotus pods, almonds, melon seeds, olive seeds, and sesame seeds. Each cake was cut into small wedges, to be enjoyed slowly with tea. Daddy always said that his father in China used to be able to cut his cake into sixteen to thirty-two wedges; one cake would last him all afternoon as he sat on his front porch to eat and drink and leisurely watch the rest of the village go by his door.

At Moon Festival time, Grandfather also called for a special rice-soup dinner for a large crowd of friends and employees. . . . A rice-soup dinner was informal and a social occasion for fun.

Yes, it was sometimes very lucky to be born a Chinese daughter. The Americans, Jade Snow heard, did not have a Moon Festival nor a seven-day New Year celebration with delicious accompaniments. Besides, they burned their Chinese firecrackers five months later on one day only— the Fourth of July!

---

6. **lotus pods** (LOH-tuhs PAHDZ) *n.* the lotus was a sacred flower to the people of Egypt, India, and China, the pods carry the lotus seeds

# AFTER YOU READ

## Exchanging Backgrounds and Cultures

1. How do the lives of the Wongs change during the Chinese New Year?

2. What does the importance of "celebrating properly" during the New Year suggest about Chinese values?

3. In this excerpt, what does Wong reveal about her attitude toward her heritage?

## What Do You Think?

Which part of this selection captured your interest most? Why was this particular aspect especially meaningful to you?

## Experiencing Nonfiction

In this autobiographical account, Wong recalls her childhood memories of a special holiday. Which holidays or family traditions would you write about if you were preparing your autobiography? Make a list of those experiences. Then pick one that you think others would find interesting. Write an autobiographical sketch that describes the way in which your family usually observes this holiday or tradition. Remember to include descriptions of the setting and the people involved.

*Optional Activity* Write a brief personal account that describes a memorable event that you have witnessed, such as a parade. Be sure to tell how the event made you feel, as well as providing vivid descriptions of the actual event. For instance, in the excerpt, Wong describes the Lion Dances and the feelings she experienced as she watched.

# UNIT 1: FOCUS ON WRITING

There are many forms of nonfiction, including biographies, essays, reports, editorials, and news stories. Although these forms vary in purpose, audience, and tone, they share elements, such as the use of facts and reasons to support main ideas. For instance, in Amy Tan's speech, "My Mother's English," she lists the books and magazines her mother reads in order to support the idea that her mother understands English perfectly.

## Writing Nonfiction

Choose one of the following nonfiction forms: biography, autobiography, news article, essay, or letter. Then, using the steps on this page, write your own piece of nonfiction.

## The Writing Process

Good writing requires both time and effort. An effective writer completes a number of stages that together make up the writing process. The stages of the writing process are given below to help guide you through your assignment.

### Prewriting

Begin by brainstorming for topics. List every idea that comes to mind. Then choose the idea that would make the most interesting nonfiction topic.

Now think about your topic. Is it too broad? You may want to use a technique called clustering to narrow your topic. Create a cluster diagram by writing your topic in the center of a page and circling it. Surround it with subtopics, and draw lines showing their connection to the topic. You can then use one of the subtopics as the focus of your piece.

Next, consider your purpose, audience, and tone, as well as the form of nonfiction you plan to use. Is your purpose to describe, to explain, or to persuade? For whom are you writing? Does your audience know a great deal about your topic or will you have to provide background information? Should you use an informal or formal tone?

Now gather facts and details about your topic. Ideas and information can come either from your own knowledge of the subject or from outside sources, such as books, magazines, films, or reference works. Be sure to record the sources of all your information.

Your next step is to organize the information that you have gathered. First, write a topic sentence that identifies the specific subject about which you are going to write. Then organize your supporting ideas into an outline or a list.

### Drafting and Revising

After you have organized your ideas, begin drafting. Allow your thoughts to flow as you draft. You will have a chance to revise your work later.

Use your prewriting notes and outline to help you arrange your topic sentence and supporting details. As you work, try not to stray too far from your original plan. However, if a good idea occurs while you are writing, include it in your draft.

When you are ready to revise, there are several things to consider. Make sure that you have clearly presented your topic and that you have supported it with facts and details. Also make sure that all your details relate directly to your topic. Eliminate any that do not. In addition, see that all sentences within each paragraph focus on a single subtopic. Finally, verify that you have presented your ideas in a logical order and that you have ended with a strong conclusion.

### Proofreading and Publishing

After you have finished revising, carefully proofread your work. Correct any errors in spelling, grammar, punctuation, and capitalization. Then make a final copy of your piece.

Consider sharing your work with your family or classmates. You can even submit it to your school's newspaper or literary magazine.

# UNIT 2
# FICTION OF THE
# CHINESE AMERICANS

**Fiction** consists of stories that are imagined, or made up. Some works of fiction are based on real people and situations. Others are formed entirely in the writer's imagination.

The two most common forms of fiction are novels and short stories. Novels are long works of fiction, involving complex plots, or sequences of events. In addition, novels generally contain a variety of settings and include many major and minor characters. They are also likely to have one or more themes, or central messages. Short stories, on the other hand, are brief works of fiction that generally have simpler plots. Often, short stories present characters in a single setting and focus on one conflict or situation in the characters' lives.

Fiction takes us to other worlds, leads us through imaginary adventures, and introduces us to interesting new people and situations. By reading the fiction of other cultures, we learn about the values, beliefs, and experiences of the people in those cultures. The first selection in this unit, an excerpt from Pardee Lowe's novel *Father and Glorious Descendant,* follows a young boy's struggle to come to terms with his Chinese American identity. The short story "The All-American Slurp," by Lensey Namioka, recounts the embarrassing and humorous mishaps of a Chinese family adjusting to American culture. In Monfoon Leong's novel, *Number One Son,* the narrator must come to terms with his role as the provider of his family as a result of his father's death. Finally, the excerpt from Laurence Yep's novel *Dragonwings* takes the reader back to an earlier time, when Chinese immigrants arrived in California in search of gold.

As you read these selections, think about how the authors use dialogue, action, and description to bring the characters, settings, and events to life.

**My Secret World.** *Asian American Arts Center.*
Painting by Martin Wong.

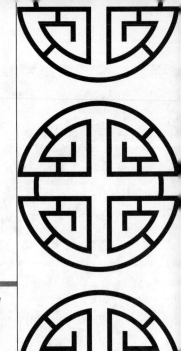

# INTRODUCTION

## Father Cures a
## Presidential Fever

Pardee Lowe, the son of Chinese immigrants, was born in California in 1905. After attending Stanford University and Harvard Business School, Lowe participated in the Chinese War Relief Organization, which supplied food and medicine to Chinese war refugees. His articles about the efforts of this organization were published in a variety of journals during the 1940s, launching his career as a writer.

The following excerpt is a chapter from Lowe's novel, *Father and Glorious Descendant*. In this book, Lowe focuses primarily on his father's struggles and hardships as a way of capturing the immigrant experience in the United States. He tells about the early days in San Francisco's Chinatown, the devastating effects of the San Francisco earthquake of 1906, and the family's move to the culturally mixed community of Belleville. In this novel, Lowe also expresses his own desire to preserve his Chinese heritage while he adapts to U.S. society. The excerpt you are about to read, "Father Cures a Presidential Fever," recounts Lowe's first encounter with discrimination.

# Father Cures a Presidential Fever

from *Father and Glorious Descendant*

by Pardee Lowe

**H**ow I came to be infected with Presidentitis even now I find somewhat difficult to explain. That it was not congenital was amply demonstrated by Father's matter-of-fact superiority over such divine foolishness. And Mother, bless her realistic Chinese soul, never affected awareness of such mundane matters until the political clubs of our neighborhood (we lived in the toughest one in East Belleville) celebrated under her very nose with torchlight parades . . . the glorious victories of their Men of the People. Whenever this happened she would exclaim, "My, my, what queer people the Americans are!"

The first time Father discovered how long the first-born man child of his household had been exposed to the ravages of this dread disease, he was horrified. "Unbelievable!" he stormed. But Mother, who had a strong will of her own, flew right back at him. And when she cried aloud, with Heaven as her witness, that she did not know how I caught it or how she could have prevented it, Father recognized the justice of her remarks. She couldn't. Kwong Chong, our own neighborhood dry-goods store, household duties, and two new babies kept Mother so harassed that she had no time to chase us about the streets or down the back alleys. Later, to still her flow of tears,

Father even grudgingly admitted his full responsibility. By moving our family to an American neighborhood, according to Mother, he had needlessly exposed us all to the malady. . . .

From Father's point of view, we children were to be raised at home according to the old and strict Chinese ideal. But in that ever-widening circle of American neighborhood life beyond the narrow confines of our home, Father had no control. A daily commuter to his shop in San Francisco's Chinatown, an hour's ride away by steam train and ferry, he was never fully apprised of our actions until too late.

He was ignorant, for instance, of what transpired in the large wooden public school situated some three short blocks from our home. He was confident we were in good hands. If he had only known what was awaiting his son there, he might not have been so eager to have me acquire an American schooling.

When at the age of five I entered the portals of this mid-Victorian architectural firetrap, surrounded by its iron-spiked fence and tall trees, for the first time, I recognized it as an international institution in which I was free to indulge my own most un-Chinese inclinations— and, unintentionally to be sure, to undermine Father's high hopes.

I can still vividly remember the strange excitement of the first morning roll call, which was to be repeated daily for many years to come. Clumsily, the teacher pronounced our names. . . .

There we stood. In the company of fifteen other beginners, no two in the entire group of the same nationality, I was embarking upon a new and glorious adventure, the educational melting pot, which was to make every one of us, beyond peradventure,[1] an American. . . .

---

1. **beyond peradventure** (per-uhd-VEN-chuhr) beyond a doubt

No sooner was Father's back turned than I would dash madly to the street line.  On my way I would stop and pick a bunch of posies from our neighbors' back yards, praying fervently[2] that I would be the only pupil waiting for Miss McIntyre, our teacher. Disappointment invariably awaited me, for I was not alone. Anna, Nancy, Penelope, and Robert, sharing exactly the same sentiments, always managed to get there ahead of me.

As soon as we spotted Miss McIntyre's tall figure alighting from the car, we sprang forward.  With a warm smile of affection which enfolded us all, she allowed us to grab her hands, snatch her books from her arms and literally drag her from the rear step of the car to the front steps of the school, happily protesting every step of the way: "Now, children! . . . Now *children!*"

Coming mainly from immigrant homes where parents were too preoccupied with earning a living to devote much time to their children, we transferred our youthful affections to this one person who had both the time and the disposition to mother us. We showered upon our white-haired teacher the blind, wholehearted loyalty of the young. Our studies we readily absorbed, not because we particularly liked them so much as because it was "she" who taught us. Thus, with the three R's, games, stories, a weekly bath which she personally administered in the school's bathroom—two pupils at a time—and her love, she whom we staunchly[3] enshrined[4] in our hearts laid the rudimentary[5] but firm foundation of our personal brand of American culture.

---

2. **fervently**  (FER-vuhnt-lee)  *adv.* passionately
3. **staunchly**  (STAWNCH-lee)  *adv.* strongly
4. **enshrine**  (ihn-SHREYEN)  *v.* to hold as sacred
5. **rudimentary**  (roo-duh-MEN-tuhr-ee)  *adj.* elementary beginnings

Then, one day it happened. Miss McIntyre, herself the daughter of an Irish immigrant who had come to California during the Gold Rush, read to us with deep emotion the life of George Washington. The virtues displayed by the Father of Our Country, particularly when confessing his act of chopping down the cherry tree, were, she led us to believe, the very ones which would, if faithfully practised, win us equal fame. Concluding the narrative, she looked in turn at Anna, Penelope, and Robert. She was challenging us to higher things. As her eyes caught mine, she added with conviction, "And every single one of you can be President of the United States someday!"

I shall never forget that occasion. . . .

Everything I did from this moment on served only to strengthen the grandiose dream whose chief interlocking threads included myself, Father, and the Presidency. Much to the disgust of my more active playmates and the envy of my bookworm friends, I became a walking encyclopedia of American history. I could repeat the full names and dates of every President of these United States. And I knew the vivid, gory details, authentic and apocryphal,[6] of every important military engagement in which Americans took part—and always victoriously. . . .

Now what would Father say?

Father, uncertain of the exact nature of the enchantment that had suddenly ensnared his son, looked at me queerly . . . . In his own mind he had worked out a series of special therapeutic treatments to counteract my desperate malady,[7] Presidentitis.

. . . Father said gently, "Glorious Descendant, how would you like to go to a private boarding school in China?"

---

**6. apocryphal** (uh-PAHK-ruh-fuhl) *adj.* not genuine, not authentic
**7. malady** (MAL-uh-dee) *n.* a sickness

I shuddered at the full significance of his suggestion. To be separated from America and from my family? And never to see them again for years and years? "No! no!" I wailed. "I don't want to go!" Rejecting the idea with all the vehemence[8] at my command, I added, "I want to stay in America!"

Father dwelt patiently on all the advantages of such a schooling but to no avail. Nothing he said moved me. What about my future, inquired Father, didn't I care? Of course, I replied, but I didn't want to be a mandarin[9] or a Chinese merchant prince at such a terrific sacrifice. Father's questions became more penetrating; they stripped the future of everything but realities. Could I, as a Chinese, ever hope to find a good job in American society? At this, I laughed. Miss McIntyre, I told him, had plainly said that I could even be President.

In these sessions, I revealed to Father the seriousness of my infection. I opened the gates to that part of my youthful life he had never known. I told him in no uncertain terms that I loved America, particularly East Belleville, which I considered to be the grandest place in all the world. Besides, I continued, why would I wish to go to China? All the things I had heard from our kinsfolk about the old country were bad, with no redeeming features. After all, I added as my clinching argument, if this were not so, why should our kinsmen wish to come to the United States?

Our cousins and uncles, Father tried desperately to explain, really wanted to stay at home with their wives and children, but because times seemed so difficult in China

---

8. **vehemence** (VEE-uh-muhns) *n.* intense feeling, strong passion
9. **mandarin** (MAN-duh-rihn) *n.* in the Chinese empire, a member of the elite

they were compelled, by economic necessity, to come and work in the Golden Mountains. "Don't think you're the only one who loves his family and hates to leave it," concluded Father somewhat angrily.

The argument became endless. The more Father pleaded, the more determined I became. America, I swore, was God's own country. It abounded in free public schools, libraries, newspapers, bathtubs, toilets, vaudeville theaters, and railroad trains. On the other hand, I reminded him, China was a place where anything might happen: One might be kidnapped, caught in a revolution, die from the heat, perish from the cold, or even pick up ringworm diseases which left huge bald patches on one's scalp.

Finally Father was convinced. Since I did not personally regard his idea with favor, trying to send me to China was hopeless. This by no means exhausted Father's (remedial) efforts on my behalf. Plan number one having failed, Father put number two into operation. He decided that if I wouldn't go to China I was to spend an extra hour each day on my Chinese studies for Tutor Chun.

Now I knew leisure no longer. My American playmates, and endless trips to the settlement library, were given up—but not forgotten. And I discovered to my painful sorrow that I had only substituted one necessary evil for another. Every evening from five to eight I (despondently) memorized, recited, and copied endless columns of queer-shaped characters which bore not the slightest resemblance to English. As I went to this school on Saturday mornings and studied my lessons on Sunday I envied Penelope, Heinz and Francisco, my poorest foreign playmates, their luxurious freedom. They did not have to learn Chinese.

Unlike my American education, my Chinese one was not crowded with success. It was not that I was entirely unwilling to learn, but simply that my brain was not ambidextrous.[10] Whenever I stood with my back to the teacher, my lips attempted to recite correctly in poetical prose Chinese history, geography or ethics, while my inner spirit was wrestling victoriously with the details of the Battle of Bunker Hill, Custer's Last Stand, or the tussle between the *Monitor* and *Merrimac.*

When it became apparent to Tutor Chun that, in spite of my extra hour a day, I was unable to balance cultural waters on both shoulders, he mercifully desisted flailing me with the bamboo duster. No amount of chastising, he informed me bitterly, would ever unravel the cultural chop suey I was making of my studies. But, in the long run, even the gentle soul of the Chinese teacher could not tolerate my muddle-headedness. One day after a particularly heart-rending recitation on my part, he telephoned Mother in despair. "Madame," he exclaimed in mortal anguish, "never have I had a pupil the equal of your son. I strain all my efforts but, alas, I profoundly regret that I am unable to teach him anything!"

Father was appalled at this news, but since he was not the kind of man who gave up easily, his determination waxed all the stronger. Subtler methods, bribery, were tried. Perhaps, he reasoned, I might develop a taste for Chinese as well as English literature if it were only made financially worth my while. Each Sunday a shining quarter would be mine, he said, if I would present him with a daily ten-minute verbal Chinese translation of the latest newspaper reports on European war developments.

Lured by this largess,[11] I made my translations. They were, to be sure, crude and swiftly drawn. But then, ten minutes was all too brief a period in which to circum-

---

**10. ambidextrous** (am-buh-DEK-struhs) *adj.* able to use both hands
   with equal ease
**11. largess** (lahr-JES) *n.* generous giving

navigate the globe and report on its current events. I endowed the military movements of von Kluck's, Foch's and Haig's armies with the élan of Sheridan's sweep down the Shenandoah, unencumbered with the intricate mechanized paraphernalia[12] of modern warfare. And long before Wilson, Clemenceau[13] and Lloyd George assembled at Versailles, I had made the map of Europe a dozen times.

Father's clever scheme not only worked, but it proved mutually beneficial. During the four years of the war, we kept it up. Thanks to the revolutionary *Young China* and the *Christian Chinese Western Daily*, he was never entirely in the dark as to which armies won which campaign and who finally won the war. Naturally, Father learned a great deal about history that wasn't so, but he did not particularly mind. I was improving my Chinese.

During this period my youthful cup of patriotism was filled to overflowing. In the first place our Americanism had finally reached the ears of the White House. The christening of my twin brothers brought two important letters of congratulation from Washington, which Father proudly framed and hung conspicuously[14] in his private office. As might be imagined, they exerted a profound influence on all our lives.

When I felt particularly in need of encouragement, I would go to the back wall of Father's office and read aloud Vice President Marshall's letter to Father. It was a human one, glowing with warmth and inspiration. There was one sentence which stood out: "To be a good American citizen, in my judgment, is about the best thing on earth, and while I cannot endow your children with any worldly goods, I can

---

12. **paraphernalia** (par-uh-fuhr-NAYL-yuh) *n. pl.* any collection of articles or equipment
13. **Clemenceau** (klay-mahn-SOH) French statesman
14. **conspicuously** (kuhn-SPIHK-yoo-wuhs-lee) *adv.* easy to see

bless them with the hope that they may grow up to be an honor to their parents and a credit to the commonwealth."

I recall this Vice-Presidential blessing so vividly because it was the (crux) of our family problem. It summed up our difficulties as well as our goal. For me, at least, it was difficult to be a filial[15] Chinese son and a good American citizen at one and the same time. For many years I used to wonder why this was so, but I appreciate now it was because I was the eldest son in what was essentially a pioneering family. Father was pioneering with Americanism—and so was I. And more often than not, we blazed entirely different trails.

When America finally entered the War, even Father's sturdy common sense softened somewhat under the heat waves of patriotism that constantly beat down upon us. I was in paradise. My youthful fancies appreciated that only strife and turmoil made heroes. When I recalled that practically every great President—Washington, Jackson, Lincoln, Grant, and Roosevelt—had once been a soldier, I bitterly lamented the fact that I was not old enough. I'd show those "Huns" (by this time I had already imbibed[16] freely at the fount of propaganda) a thing or two, I informed Father. But Father only snorted something about waiting until I could shoulder a gun, and studying Chinese.

The next summer, my thirteenth, I decided to go to work during vacation. I needed spending money badly for my first term of high school. Father applauded this show of independence until I informed him that I intended, if possible, to become an office boy in an American business firm. Then he was seized with profound misgivings. "Would they hire you?" Father inquired.

---

15. **filial** (FIHL-ee-uhl) *adj.* expected of a son or daughter
16. **imbibed** (ihm-BEYEBD) *v.* absorbed, drunk

Why shouldn't they, I replied, with overweening self-confidence. "See!" I pointed to the Sunday editions of the *San Francisco Chronicle*. "I can hold any of these jobs."

Father looked at the classified advertisements I had checked. Whether he knew what all the abbreviations meant, I wasn't certain. I didn't, but that was totally immaterial. The world was new. I was young, and for $40 a month I was willing to learn the ins. or exp. bus., work for good opps., be ready to asst. on files, and, for good measure, do gen. off. wk. for perm. adv.

Father remarked that he wasn't so certain that the millennium[17] had arrived, but he was open to conviction. He agreed to let me proceed on one condition: If I failed to find a job I was to return to Tutor Chun and study my Chinese lessons faithfully.

Blithely one sunny July morning I went forth job hunting, well-scrubbed, wearing my Sunday suit and totally unaware of the difficulties that confronted me. In my pocket were ten clipped newspaper advertisements, each one, I thought, with a job purposely made for me.

I took out the most promising one. It was for seven enterp. boys, between the ages of 12 and 16; and they were wanted at once for a bond house which offered good opps. as well as $50 per month. The address was on California Street.

Stopping in front of an imposing marble palace of San Francisco finance, I compared the address with the clipping. It checked. How simply grand it would be to work for such a firm, I thought, as the elevator majestically pulled us up to the ninth floor. I trembled with eager anticipation as I pushed open the glass door of Richards and Mathison, for it seemed as though a new world were swimming into view.

---

17. **millennium** (mih-LEN-ee-uhm) *n.* a period of great happiness, peace, and prosperity

"Wad-a-ya-wunt?" barked the sharp voice of a young lady. I looked in her direction. There she sat behind a shiny, thin brass cage, just like a bank teller—or a monkey, for above her head hung a sign. It read INFORMATION.

"Please, ma'am," I asked, "can you tell me where I can find Mr. Royal?"

"Humph!" she snorted, as she looked me up and down as if to say I didn't have a chance. "He's busy, you'll have to wait."

After what seemed hours, the girl threw open the office gate and motioned me to enter. I followed her down a long aisle of desks, every one as large as a kitchen table. At each desk sat a man or a girl shuffling large cards or scribbling on long sheets of paper. As we passed, they stopped their work and looked at me queerly. I noticed several boys of my own age putting their heads together. I knew they were talking about me. And when they snickered, I wanted to punch their noses.

Opening a door marked PRIVATE, the girl announced: "Mr. Royal, here is another boy." He raised his head.

There it was. On Mr. Royal's lean, smooth-shaven face was the same look of incredulity that I had once noticed on Mr. Brown's. But only for a moment. For he suddenly reached for a cigarette, lit it and looked at me quizzically, while I hopped on one foot and then on the other.

"Young man," he said, "I understand you would like to work for us? Well then, you'd better tell us something of yourself."

"Why, of course," I said, "of course." And impulsively I told everything: all about my graduation from grammar school, my boy-scout training, and my desire to earn my own keep during the summer.

Mr. Royal seemed visibly impressed. When a faint smile replaced his frown, I stopped fidgeting. I fully expected him to ask me to come to work in the morning. Therefore, I was appalled when he told me that he was sorry, but all the jobs were taken. It never occurred to me that our interview would end like this.

My face fell. I hadn't expected such an answer. To soften the blow, Mr. Royal added that if I filled out an application he would call me if there were any openings.

I filled out the application under the unsympathetic eyes of the information girl, and stumbled miserably out of the office, vaguely sensible of the fact that there would never be any opening.

The feeling was intensified as I made the round of the other nine firms. Everywhere I was greeted with perturbation,[18] amusement, pity or irritation—and always with identically the same answer. "Sorry," they invariably said, "the position has just been filled." My (jaunty) self-confidence soon wilted. I sensed that something was radically, fundamentally wrong. It just didn't seem possible that overnight all of the positions could have been occupied, particularly not when everybody spoke of a labor shortage. Suspicion began to dawn. What had Father said? "American firms do not customarily employ Chinese." To verify his statement, I looked again in the newspaper the next morning and for the week after and, sure enough, just as I expected, the same ten ads were still in the newspaper.

For another week, I tried my luck. By now I was thoroughly shell-shocked. What had begun as a glorious adventure had turned into a hideous, long-drawn nightmare.

Father during this trying period wisely said nothing. Then, one morning, he dusted off my dog-eared paperbound Chinese textbooks. When I came to breakfast I found them on my desk, mute but eloquent reminders of my promise. I looked at them disconsolately.[19] A bargain was a bargain.

---

18. **perturbation** (per-tuhr-BAY-shuhn) *n*. alarm, annoyance
19. **disconsolately** (dihs-KAHN-suh-liht-lee) *adv*. cheerlessly, disappointedly

When our clock struck nine, I picked up my bundle of books. Fortunately for me, Father had already commuted to work. Only Mother saw me off. Patting me sympathetically on the shoulder, she regarded me reflectively. It was an invitation for me to unburden my heart. But not even for her would I confess my full recovery from a nearly fatal disease. That moment was reserved for my long walk to language school.

I marched out of the house insouciant.[20] When I wasn't whistling I was muttering to myself a Jewish slang phrase I had just picked up. It was "Ishkabibble" and it meant that I didn't care. And I didn't until I reached the park where all my most vivid daydreaming periods were spent. There, I broke down and wept. For the first time I admitted to myself the cruel truth—I didn't have a "Chinaman's chance" of becoming President of the United States. In this crash of the lofty hopes which Miss McIntyre had raised, it did not occur to me to reflect that the chances of Francisco Trujillo, Yuri Matsuyama, or Penelope Lincoln were actually no better than mine. But after a good cry I felt better—anyway, I could go to an American school again in the fall.

---

20. **insouciant** (ihn-SOO-see-uhnt) *adj.* calm and untroubled

# AFTER YOU READ

## Exchanging Backgrounds and Cultures

1. What does Lowe's childhood ambition to be President of the United States suggest about his perception of himself?

2. Why do you think Lowe's father is upset about his son's ambition? What does this reveal about Lowe's father's attitude toward U.S. society and toward his Chinese heritage?

3. What does Lowe learn about U.S. society during his job search? How does this experience change his sense of identity?

## What Do You Think?

Which character or situation in this excerpt did you find most interesting? Why was it especially meaningful for you?

## Experiencing Fiction

This chapter from Lowe's novel presents a situation in which the narrator is forced to alter his view of himself and society. Think about an experience that you have had that either changed, or made you aware of, your own sense of identity. Then write a fictional narrative based on that experience. Use the impact that the experience had on you to develop the theme, or main point, of the narrative.

*Optional Activity* Write a story about a character who has a strong ambition. What conflicts does this character confront and overcome to achieve his or her dream? Remember to develop the character through his or her own thoughts, dialogue, and actions.

## *INTRODUCTION*
## The All-American Slurp

Lensey Namioka was born in Peking, China, in 1929. She moved to the United States as a child with her father, a linguist, and her mother, a doctor. After completing graduate school in California, Namioka spent many years as a mathematics teacher. In the 1970s, she began to write travel books and humorous articles for newspapers and magazines, later turning to fiction. As a writer, she draws heavily on both her background and that of her husband, who was raised in the town of Himeji, Japan. Namioka's own knowledge of Japanese culture originated during her childhood while her mother was in Japan.

Namioka's most popular books center on Zenta and Matsuzo, two young samurai warriors living in Japan. These adventure tales were inspired by her husband's family history. The story you are about to read, "The All-American Slurp," is very different in content and tone. This story is based on Namioka's own experiences when she and her parents first arrived in the United States. In the story, she reveals the funny, and often painfully embarrassing, situations her family endured as they adjusted to a new culture.

# The All-American Slurp

by Lensey Namioka

The first time our family was invited out to dinner in America, we disgraced ourselves while eating celery. We had emigrated to this country from China, and during our early days here we had a hard time with American table manners.

In China we never ate celery raw, or any other kind of vegetable raw. We always had to disinfect[1] the vegetables in boiling water first. When we were presented with our first relish[2] tray, the raw celery caught us unprepared.

We had been invited to dinner by our neighbors, the Gleasons. After arriving at the house, we shook hands with our hosts and packed ourselves into a sofa. As our family of four sat stiffly in a row, my younger brother and I stole glances at our parents for a clue as to what to do next.

Mrs. Gleason offered the relish tray to Mother. The tray looked pretty, with its tiny red radishes, curly sticks of carrots, and long, slender stalks of pale green celery. "Do try some of the celery, Mrs. Lin," she said. "It's from a local farmer, and it's sweet."

---

1. **disinfect** (dihs-ihn-FECT) *v.* sterilize
2. **relish** (REL-ihsh) *n.* any of a variety of foods, such as pickles, olives, and raw vegetables, served as an appetizer

Mother picked up one of the green stalks, and Father followed suit. Then I picked up a stalk, and my brother did too. So there we sat, each with a stalk of celery in our right hand.

Mrs. Gleason kept smiling. "Would you like to try some of the dip, Mrs. Lin? It's my own recipe: sour cream and onion flakes, with a dash of Tabasco sauce."

Most Chinese don't care for dairy products, and in those days I wasn't even ready to drink fresh milk. Sour cream sounded perfectly revolting. Our family shook our heads in unison.

Mrs. Gleason went off with the relish tray to the other guests, and we carefully watched to see what they did. Everyone seemed to eat the raw vegetables quite happily.

Mother took a bite of her celery. *Crunch.* "It's not bad!" she whispered.

Father took a bite of his celery. *Crunch.* "Yes, it *is* good," he said, looking surprised.

I took a bite, and then my brother. *Crunch, crunch.* It was more than good; it was delicious. Raw celery has a slight sparkle, a zingy taste that you don't get in cooked celery. When Mrs. Gleason came around with the relish tray, we each took another stalk of celery, except my brother. He took two.

There was only one problem: long strings ran through the length of the stalk, and they got caught in my teeth. When I help my mother in the kitchen, I always pull the strings out before slicing celery.

I pulled the strings out of my stalk. *Z-z-zip, z-z-zip.* My brother followed suit. *Z-z-zip, z-z-zip, z-z-zip.* To my left, my parents were taking care of their own stalks. *Z-z-zip, z-z-zip, z-z-zip.*

Suddenly I realized that there was dead silence except for our zipping. Looking up, I saw that the eyes of everyone in the room were on our family. Mr. and Mrs. Gleason, their daughter Meg, who was my friend, and their neighbors the Badels—they were all staring at us as we busily pulled the strings of our celery.

That wasn't the end of it. Mrs. Gleason announced that dinner was served and invited us to the dining table. It was lavishly covered with platters of food, but we couldn't see any chairs around the table. So we helpfully carried over some dining chairs and sat down. All the other guests just stood there.

Mrs. Gleason bent down and whispered to us, "This is a buffet dinner. You help yourselves to some food and eat it in the living room."

Our family beat a retreat back to the sofa as if chased by enemy soldiers. For the rest of the evening, too mortified to go back to the dining table, I nursed a bit of potato salad on my plate.

Next day Meg and I got on the school bus together. I wasn't sure how she would feel about me after the spectacle our family made at the party. But she was just the same as usual, and the only reference she made to the party was, "Hope you and your folks got enough to eat last night. You certainly didn't take very much. Mom never tries to figure out how much food to prepare. She just puts everything on the table and hopes for the best."

I began to relax. The Gleasons' dinner party wasn't so different from a Chinese meal after all. My mother also puts everything on the table and hopes for the best.

Meg was the first friend I had made after we came to America. I eventually got acquainted with a few other kids in school, but Meg was still the only real friend I had.

My brother didn't have any problems with making friends. He spent all his time with some boys who were teaching him baseball, and in no time he could speak English much faster than I could—not better, but faster.

I worried more about making mistakes, and I spoke carefully, making sure I could say everything right before opening my mouth. At least I had a better accent than my parents, who never really got rid of their Chinese accent, even years later. My parents had both studied English in school before coming to America, but what they had studied was mostly written English, not spoken.

Father's approach to English was a scientific one. Since Chinese verbs have no tense, he was fascinated by the way English verbs changed form according to whether they were in the present, past imperfect, perfect, pluperfect, future, or future perfect tense. He was always making diagrams of verbs and their inflections,[3] and he looked for opportunities to show off his mastery of the pluperfect and future perfect tenses, his two favorites. "I shall have finished my project by Monday," he would say smugly.

Mother's approach was to memorize lists of polite phrases that would cover all possible social situations. She was constantly muttering things like "I'm fine, thank you. And you?" Once she accidentally stepped on someone's foot, and hurriedly blurted, "Oh, that's quite all right!" Embarrassed by her slip, she resolved to do better next time. So when someone stepped on *her* foot, she cried, "You're welcome!"

In our own different ways, we made progress in learning English. But I had another worry, and that was my appearance. My brother didn't have to worry, since Mother bought him blue jeans for school, and he dressed like all the other boys. But she insisted that girls had to wear skirts. By the time she saw that Meg and the other girls were wearing jeans, it was too late. My school clothes were bought already, and we didn't have money left to buy new outfits for me. We had too many other things to buy first, like furniture, pots, and pans.

---

3. **inflections** (ihn-FLEK-shuhnz) *n.* any changes in tone or pitch of the voice

The first time I visited Meg's house, she took me upstairs to her room, and I wound up trying on her clothes. We were pretty much the same size, since Meg was shorter and thinner than average. Maybe that's how we became friends in the first place. Wearing Meg's jeans and T-shirt, I looked at myself in the mirror. I could almost pass for an American—from the back, anyway. At least the kids in school wouldn't stop and stare at me in the hallways, which was what they did when they saw me in my white blouse and navy blue skirt that went a couple of inches below the knees.

When Meg came to my house, I invited her to try on my Chinese dresses, the ones with a high collar and slits up the sides. Meg's eyes were bright as she looked at herself in the mirror. She struck several sultry poses, and we nearly fell over laughing.

The dinner party at the Gleasons' didn't stop my growing friendship with Meg. Things were getting better for me in other ways too. Mother finally bought me some jeans at the end of the month, when Father got his paycheck. She wasn't in any hurry about buying them at first, until I worked on her. This is what I did. Since we didn't have a car in those days, I often ran down to the neighborhood store to pick up things for her. The groceries cost less at a big supermarket, but the closest one was many blocks away. One day, when she ran out of flour, I offered to borrow a bike from our neighbor's son and buy a ten-pound bag of flour at the big supermarket. I mounted the boy's bike and waved to Mother. "I'll be back in five minutes!"

Before I started pedaling, I heard her voice behind me. "You can't go out in public like that! People can see all the way up to your thighs!"

"I'm sorry," I said innocently. "I thought you were in a hurry to get the flour." For dinner we were going to have pot-stickers (fried Chinese dumplings), and we needed a lot of flour.

"Couldn't you borrow a girl's bicycle?" complained Mother. "That way your skirt won't be pushed up."

"There aren't too many of those around," I said. "Almost all the girls wear jeans while riding a bike, so they don't see any point in buying a girl's bike."

We didn't eat pot-stickers that evening, and Mother was thoughtful. Next day we took the bus downtown and she bought me a pair of jeans. In the same week, my brother made the baseball team of his junior high school, Father started taking driving lessons, and Mother discovered rummage sales.[4] We soon got all the furniture we needed, plus a dart board and a 1,000-piece jigsaw puzzle (fourteen hours later, we discovered that it was a 999-piece jigsaw puzzle). There was hope that the Lins might become a normal American family after all.

Then came our dinner at the Lakeview restaurant.

The Lakeview was an expensive restaurant, one of those places where a headwaiter dressed in tails conducted you to your seat, and the only light came from candles and flaming desserts. In one corner of the room a lady harpist played tinkling melodies.

Father wanted to celebrate, because he had just been promoted. He worked for an electronics company, and after his English started improving, his superiors decided to appoint him to a position more suited to his training. The promotion not only brought a higher salary but was also a tremendous boost to his pride.

Up to then we had eaten only in Chinese restaurants. Although my brother and I were becoming fond of hamburgers, my parents didn't care much for western food, other than chow mein.[5]

---

4. **rummage sales** (RUM-ihj SAYLZ) *n.* sales of a variety of donated articles, used or new
5. **chow mein** (chow MAYN) a Chinese American dish: a thick meat stew flavored with soy sauce

But this was a special occasion, and Father asked his coworkers to recommend a really elegant restaurant. So there we were at the Lakeview, stumbling after the headwaiter in the murky dining room.

At our table we were handed our menus, and they were so big that to read mine I almost had to stand up again. But why bother? It was mostly in French, anyway.

Father, being an engineer, was always systematic. He took out a pocket French dictionary. "They told me that most of the items would be in French, so I came prepared." He even had a pocket flashlight, the size of a marking pen. While Mother held the flashlight over the menu, he looked up the items that were in French.

"*Pâté en croûte,*" he muttered. "Let's see . . . *pâté* is paste. . . . *croûte* is crust . . . hmm . . . a paste in crust."

The waiter stood looking patient. I squirmed and died at least fifty times.

At long last Father gave up. "Why don't we just order four complete dinners at random?" he suggested.

"Isn't that risky?" asked Mother. "The French eat some rather peculiar things, I've heard."

"A Chinese can eat anything a Frenchman can eat," Father declared.

The soup arrived in a plate. How do you get soup up from a plate? I glanced at the other diners, but the ones at the nearby tables were not on their soup course, while the more distant ones were invisible in the darkness.

Fortunately my parents had studied books on western etiquette[6] before they came to America. "Tilt your plate," whispered my mother. "It's easier to spoon the soup up that way."

She was right. Tilting the plate did the trick. But the etiquette book didn't say anything about what you did after the soup reached your lips. As any respectable Chinese

---

6. **etiquette** (ET-ih-kuht)  *n.* manners, ways of behaving

knows, the correct way to eat your soup is to slurp. This helps to cool the liquid and prevent you from burning your lips. It also shows your appreciation.

We showed our appreciation. *Shloop,* went my father. *Shloop,* went my mother. *Shloop, shloop,* went my brother, who was the hungriest.

The lady harpist stopped playing to take a rest. And in the silence, our family's consumption of soup suddenly seemed unnaturally loud. You know how it sounds on a rocky beach when the tide goes out and the water drains from all those little pools? They go *shloop, shloop, shloop.* That was the Lin family, eating soup.

At the next table a waiter was pouring wine. When a large *shloop* reached him, he froze. The bottle continued to pour, and red wine flooded the tabletop and into the lap of a customer. Even the customer didn't notice anything at first, being also hypnotized by the *shloop, shloop, shloop.*

It was too much. "I need to go to the toilet," I mumbled, jumping to my feet. A waiter, sensing my urgency, quickly directed me to the ladies' room.

I splashed cold water on my burning face, and as I dried myself with a paper towel, I stared into the mirror. In this perfumed ladies' room, with its pink-and-silver wallpaper and marbled sinks, I looked completely out of place. What was I doing here? What was our family doing in the Lakeview restaurant? In America?

The door to the ladies' room opened. A woman came in and glanced curiously at me. I retreated into one of the toilet cubicles and latched the door.

Time passed—maybe half an hour. Then I heard the door open again, and my mother's voice. "Are you in there? You're not sick, are you?"

There was real concern in her voice. A girl can't leave her family just because they slurp their soup. Besides, the toilet cubicle had a few drawbacks as a permanent residence. "I'm all right," I said, undoing the latch.

Mother didn't tell me how the rest of the dinner went, and I didn't want to know. In the weeks following, I managed to push the whole thing into the back of my mind, where it jumped out at me only a few times a day. Even now, I turn hot all over when I think of the Lakeview restaurant.

But by the time we had been in this country for three months, our family was definitely making progress toward becoming Americanized. I remember my parents' first PTA meeting. Father wore a neat suit and tie, and Mother put on her first pair of high heels. She stumbled only once. They met my homeroom teacher and beamed as she told them that I would make honor roll soon at the rate I was going. Of course Chinese etiquette forced Father to say that I was a very stupid girl and Mother to protest that the teacher was showing favoritism toward me. But I could tell they were both very proud.

The day came when my parents announced that they wanted to give a dinner party. We had invited Chinese friends to eat with us before, but this dinner was going to be different. In addition to a Chinese-American family, we were going to invite the Gleasons.

"Gee, I can hardly wait to have dinner at your house," Meg said to me. "I just *love* Chinese food."

That was a relief. Mother was a good cook, but I wasn't sure if people who ate sour cream would also eat chicken gizzards stewed in soy sauce.

Mother decided not to take a chance with chicken gizzards. Since we had western guests, she set the table with large dinner plates, which we never used in Chinese meals. In fact we didn't use individual plates at all, but picked up food from the platters in the middle of the table and brought it directly to our rice bowls. Following the practice of Chinese-American restaurants, Mother also placed large serving spoons on the platters.

The dinner started well. Mrs. Gleason exclaimed at the beautifully arranged dishes of food: the colorful candied fruit in the sweet-and-sour pork dish, the noodle-thin shreds of chicken meat stir-fried with tiny peas, and the glistening pink prawns[7] in a ginger sauce.

At first I was too busy enjoying my food to notice how the guests were doing. But soon I remembered by duties. Sometimes guests were too polite to help themselves and you had to serve them with more food.

I glanced at Meg, to see if she needed more food, and my eyes nearly popped out at the sight of her plate. It was piled with food: the sweet-and-sour meat pushed right against the chicken shreds, and the chicken sauce ran into the prawns. She had been taking food from a second dish before she finished eating her helping from the first!

Horrified, I turned to look at Mrs. Gleason. She was dumping rice out of her bowl and putting it on her dinner plate. Then she ladled prawns and gravy on top of the rice and mixed everything together, the way you mix sand, gravel, and cement to make concrete.

I couldn't bear to look any longer, and I turned to Mr. Gleason. He was chasing a pea around his plate. Several times he got it to the edge, but when he tried to pick it up with his chopsticks, it rolled back toward the center of the plate again. Finally he put down his chopsticks and picked up the pea with his fingers. He really did! A grown man!

All of us, our family and the Chinese guests, stopped eating to watch the activities of the Gleasons. I wanted to giggle. Then I caught my mother's eyes on me. She frowned and shook her head slightly, and I understood the message: the Gleasons were not used to Chinese ways, and they were just coping the best they could. For some reason I thought of celery strings.

---

**7. prawns** (PRAWNZ) *n. pl.* a kind of shrimp

When the main courses were finished, Mother brought out a platter of fruit. "I hope you weren't expecting a sweet dessert," she said. "Since the Chinese don't eat dessert, I didn't think to prepare any."

"Oh, I couldn't possibly eat dessert!" cried Mrs. Gleason. "I'm simply stuffed!"

Meg had different ideas. When the table was cleared, she announced that she and I were going for a walk. "I don't know about you, but I feel like dessert," she told me, when we were outside. "Come on, there's a Dairy Queen down the street. I could use a big chocolate milkshake!"

Although I didn't really want anything more to eat, I insisted on paying for the milkshakes. After all, I was still hostess.

Meg got her large chocolate milkshake and I had a small one. Even so, she was finishing hers while I was only half done. Toward the end she pulled hard on her straws and went *shloop, shloop.*

"Do you always slurp when you eat a milkshake?" I asked, before I could stop myself.

Meg grinned. "Sure. All Americans slurp."

# AFTER YOU READ

## Exchanging Backgrounds and Cultures

1. What does the narrator learn through her friendship with Meg?

2. How do the depictions of the dinner parties highlight the differences between Chinese and American cultures?

3. What does this selection reveal about Namioka's attitude toward her cultural heritage? What does it suggest about her attitude toward American society?

## What Do You Think?

Which character or scene in this short story was especially meaningful to you? Did it remind you of a personal experience that you have had? Explain.

## Experiencing Fiction

In this story, Namioka recounts many funny and embarrassing situations she and her family experienced as they adjusted to American culture. Have you ever found yourself in an embarrassing situation? What were the circumstances of the experience? Write a short story that conveys this encounter. Like Namioka, use humor and surprise to make the story interesting for your readers.

*Optional Activity* Write a short story that describes a special friendship between two people from different cultures. Base the story on one of your own friendships or on the relationship of two imaginary characters. In your story, illustrate what each character learns about the other's culture.

# INTRODUCTION
## from Number One Son

Monfoon Leong, born in San Diego's Chinatown in 1916, was the eldest son in a large Chinese American family. When he was 14, his father died. In keeping with Chinese tradition, Leong assumed the role of head of the household and took a job to support his mother and younger brothers and sisters. Because of his enormous responsibilities at such a young age, Leong began to identify with his parents' generation. He became interested in his cultural background and enjoyed learning about Chinese customs, traditions, superstitions, and folktales.

As a Chinese American, Leong was unusual for his time because he happily embraced his traditional Chinese heritage while readily adapting to American society. His talent as a writer was recognized by his English professors at San Jose State College and Stanford University. However, his stories were not published until well after his death in 1964. Based largely on Leong's own experiences, his fiction often examines the conflicts between Chinese and American cultures. In the following story, "Number One Son," a Chinese American boy struggles to overcome his resentment about assuming his traditional role as head of the family upon his father's death.

# from *Number One Son*

by Monfoon Leong

In a few minutes Ming would be home. Slumped in his seat, he glared out of the window as the suburban bus jerked and shook its way through the downtown traffic. The usual hurrying shoppers pushed along, arms filled with packages; the usual harried policemen watched over the intersections; the usual drivers inched through the crowds to make their turns. All were preoccupied with the business of shopping for Christmas.

Ming wondered, and reproached himself even as he wondered, if he really cared any more than those strangers did that his father died. This father of his had been little more than an old man with iron-gray hair that he saw occasionally on his Sunday trips home. Then it was nearly always only, "Hello, Pa," answered by an almost inaudible grunt as the old man hurried in from the restaurant to spend his two-hour rest period in bed. The dishwashing was bad for his rheumatism,[1] Ming had heard him say many times, but you had to work when there were six children and a woman to feed. Really, there were only five

---

1. **rheumatism** (ROO-muh-tihzm) *n.* a widely used term to describe swellings or stiffness of the joints and muscles

since Ming was out working as a houseboy,[2] but Ming had never corrected him. Now he was dead.

Ming braced himself against the window ledge as the bus turned a corner and headed toward Chinatown. He wondered if Mrs. Warner would be able to take care of the house and the twins without him. The twins, a pair of hellions,[3] were only eight, but they were nearly as tall as Ming, and he was fifteen. He had planned to teach them to play football. There was always a little time right after school before he had to start helping with the preparation of dinner. He saw again the three square boxes under their Christmas tree. Two helmets and a football, probably. He caught himself wishing that his father could buy him a football helmet and he shut the Warners from his mind. His father could never buy him anything. He should be grieving, but all he could feel was a harsh resentment against the man who had been hardly aware of his existence and who had just left him with a family to support.

He deposited a dime in the coin box and got off the bus to walk the one block to his home. . . .

A half dozen of the neighborhood boys were playing football in the street. They stopped their playing to let a car go by and saw Ming. One of the boys yelled "Come on, —" but stopped short when one of the others whispered fiercely into his ear. Ming raised his hand in greeting, but said nothing. They very carefully ignored him and started playing again.

"Home" for Ming was in a long, one-story building running the entire length of the block. Set at regular intervals in the once-whitewashed plaster wall that faced the street were screen doors, each flanked by a large, screened window. Most of the screens were brown with rust and

---

2. **houseboy** (HOWS-boi) *n.* a boy hired to do cleaning or other everyday chores in a home or hotel
3. **hellions** (HEL-yuhnz) *n.* mischievous troublemakers

sagging gently in their frames. Ming stopped at the third door from the corner and pulled it open. He stepped directly into his front room, for the heavy inner door was open.

The entire family was in the small room. He knew that his mother must have gathered them together to await his coming. On the worn, faded couch that squatted in front of the window sat his brothers, the three youngest of the family. All three turned identically serious faces toward him as he walked in, faces whose subdued quality was strained and unfamiliar, almost ludicrous.[4] The younger of his sisters, sitting near the end of the couch in a straight-backed chair with her thin, brown legs wrapped around those of the chair, looked as if she were about to burst into tears. The other was seated with their mother opposite the boys. She held her mother's hand in both of hers and was looking anxiously up into her face.

His mother's eyes were dull with a lifeless opaqueness,[5] their lids red and puffy. Her fleshless cheeks were tightly drawn, her lips set in a line of resignation. Ming wanted to run to his mother, to throw his arms around her to ease the pain of her grief, but his Chinese childhood and years of working as a houseboy had taught him to restrain his impulses. If he did hold her in his arms, he would not know what to say to console her. He did not know the proper Chinese words. He took a few steps toward her and stood mute for a few moments, searching for something to say. Then he said quietly and deliberately in his mother's Cantonese[6] dialect, "Papa . . . when die?"

She opened her mouth, closed it again and swallowed hard, then said hoarsely, "Last night. I wait till morning to call you. Not want to wake up your boss."

---

4. **ludicrous** (LOO-dih-krus) *adj.* absurd, ridiculous
5. **opaqueness** (oh-PAYK-nuhs) *n.* not easily understood
6. **Cantonese** (kan-tuh-NEEZ) *adj.* the way people speak who live in Canton, China

Poor Mother, Ming thought. Afraid he'd lose his job? The pay wouldn't be enough to take care of the family. He said, "Papa is where now?"

"At funeral parlor. Last night they took him there."

"Did you not call doctor?"

"Papa died before he came. Doctor said, heart had something wrong." She paused, then added, "Papa gone now, Ming. You are number one son, now head of family."

She needn't have told Ming that. He had heard often of the old custom. Even his mother was to abide by his decisions now. He looked around at his brothers and sisters and felt the circle closing in about his life, tying it in chains of traditional responsibility. He felt his jaw tighten. It was his father who had begotten this big brood,[7] his father who could barely earn enough to keep them alive, his father who had left the empty rice bowls for him to fill, his father who had given him nothing. He wanted to curse his father and did not dare. There would be no more school for him. He would have to work full time now to support his father's children. He had been told in school that his I.Q. was high. What good was a high I.Q. when he would not be able to finish high school, much less even dream of college? Damn the Chinese custom. He was an American. He had the right to leave the family and pursue his own happiness. . . .

"Ming?" The voice at the door was a familiar one.

"Come in, Grandfather Choak," he said, trying to hide the tremor in his voice.

The door opened with a creak and a short, round man entered. He looked like nothing more or less than a Buddha[8] in an American business suit. Ming had always called the man "Grandfather" although they were not actually related in any way. It was customary because he

---

7. **brood** (BROOD) *n.* all the children in the family

8. **Buddha** (BŌOD-uh) *n.* a religious philosopher who lived in India 563?-483? B.C. and founded Buddhism

was of the same clan as Ming's mother and had come from the same village in China. To Ming, he had always been no less than a real grandfather.

The old man glanced quickly at all the family, but addressed himself only to Ming in his mother's dialect. "Ming," he said very solemnly, "your father leave no money. We must get money from friends for funeral. You come with me."

"I must go?" Ming started to turn toward his mother as he said it.

"You are head of family," Grandfather Choak said.

Ming started to frame a denial, but under Grandfather Choak's placid gaze, he stopped himself and said, "Yes, I go with you." He followed the old man to the door, but stopped and said, "My Chinese not very good. I won't know what to say to people."

"I talk for you."

They stopped first at Kwon Kim's herb store. Kwon Kim was weighing out some bear gall[9] for a customer. Ming watched the wizened[10] old herbalist[11] behind the counter as he carefully placed a whole gall bladder on the pan of his balance and peered over his glasses to read the weight. Ming remembered that Kwon Kim had always grumbled when the kids had come in the store to beg for the sweet prunes that were kept in a huge jar on the counter. They were only to be used by his customers to take the bitter taste of his herb teas from their mouths, Kwon Kim had said. The memory of the man's miserliness made Ming very uneasy and he found himself wishing that Grandfather Choak had decided to start with someone else.

When Kwon Kim had finished with his customer, he

9. **bear gall** (BAIR GAWL) *n.* the gall bladder of a bear was once used in China as a medicine
10. **wizened** (WIHZ-uhnd) *adj.* wrinkled
11. **herbalist** (ER-buhl-ihst) *n.* someone who grows, collects, or sells certain kinds of seed plants

turned to Ming and Grandfather Choak. He clucked his tongue and said, "Very sorry your father pass beyond, Ming. Leave big family for you."

Ming strained for the words to reply. Grandfather Choak cleared his throat and said, "Father of Ming leave no money, Kim." The herbalist cocked his head over to one side for a moment as if to let the statement drain from his ear to his mind. Then, without a word, he pulled out a drawer behind the counter, picked up a bill, and dropped it on the counter, shaking his head and muttering, "Too bad. Too bad."

While Grandfather Choak pulled a pencil and a tablet of rice paper[12] from his coat pocket and started writing some characters in the tablet, Ming stared at the bill on the counter. It was a twenty. And Grandfather Choak had not even asked Kwon Kim for money. Kwon Kim was speaking.

"Father of Ming was good father," he said. "Every day I saw him go by carrying bag of cakes for children."

It was true. Ming had forgotten. His father had unfailingly brought home a bag of cakes from the restaurant when he returned for his afternoon nap. But they couldn't live on those cakes now.

He thanked Kwon Kim and followed Grandfather Choak out. The Buddha-like man waddled down the street with Ming at his side and turned into a new, self-service grocery. Flaunting its modernity, shiny gold letters on the big front window announced, "Chung's Super Market." Grandfather Choak went directly to the well-fed-looking young man who was presiding over the cash register. There was no mistaking the Mr. Chung of "Chung's Super Market."

Before Grandfather Choak had finished telling of the need of Ming's family, Mr. Chung snorted, "Man is fool to have such big family when cannot make enough money for

---

12. **rice paper** (REYES PAY-puhr) *n.* a thin paper made from the straw of rice grass

them." He looked hard at Ming. "Young man must face truth about father. He was failure as father and failure as man. Must depend on others even when he is dead. I would be fool to give money."

Ming felt his heart pounding in his throat and choking him and his fists doubled up, ready to lash out at the face with its upper lip curled over white teeth in a self-righteous grimace. He sucked in his breath with a sob when Grandfather Choak took his arm and said, "Come."

As they turned to go, Chung said, "Wait," rang up a "No Sale" on the register and drew out a five dollar bill which he tossed on the counter. "Here."

Grandfather Choak picked it up without a word and made a note in his tablet.

"Don't take it, Grandfather Choak," Ming forced out through his clenched teeth.

"Must pay for funeral, Ming." He put a hand on Ming's shoulder before he could say anything more and urged him out of the store.

On the sidewalk, the anger oozed quickly out of Ming, leaving him weighted with a great weariness. He unclenched his fists. "He was right, Grandfather Choak," he said. "My father was a failure."

"Do not talk that way about your father."

"But he was. Family lives in hole in wall, goes without so many things other people have. Mother washes all our clothes with washboard and tub. You know I have worked since I was nine years old." All the resentment of years began to boil out of Ming. He stuttered and stumbled over the words that had to be torn up from his Chinese vocabulary, but they had to come out. "Father had no love for me. Hardly knew he had eldest son."

Grandfather Choak again put his hand on Ming's shoulder and stopped him. "Your father did best he could, Ming. Came from China without education, without English. What could he do? Raised fine, healthy family. Loved his children."

Ming's lips squeezed together. "Father loved children? He did not know what love is."

They glared into each other's eyes for a long time. Then Grandfather Choak said gently, "You go home, Ming. Perhaps it will be better if I go see others by self." He patted Ming's arm and waddled off. Ming watched him go up the street, then he turned and started homeward.

From babyhood he had been taught to respect the words of his elders. Always he had had an especially profound respect for the wisdom of Grandfather Choak, but he felt sure that Grandfather Choak was dead wrong now. Perhaps his father had tried, but trying wasn't enough. He thought of Mr. Warner's home, the football helmets. His father had not given him even the love of a father. And now he was expected to revere his memory, to take his place, to give up his chance for an education, to struggle and go down as had his father. They had no right to ask it of him.

He was about to pass the Widow Loo without speaking when she gripped his arm. "Ming Kwong!" she said. "How tall are you now." She was a dumpy woman of about forty, several inches shorter than Ming. The note of surprise dropped from her voice as she continued, "I heard about your father. Am so very sorry. Your father fine man."

She released Ming's arm to fish in a well-worn purse she was carrying. "Many times your father helped me and children. He had little money but much heart." She pulled two crumpled bills from her purse and put them into Ming's hand. "I know he did not leave you much," she said. "Maybe this will help a little."

Ming whispered a "Thank you" and she bustled away. He looked at the two one dollar bills in his hand for a long while.

His mother was anxiously waiting at the door for him. "Ming, your father's watch. They took it with him last night. We must get it back."

"Watch? Of what importance is watch? We can get it back at any time."

"No. It is gold watch your father had for many years.

Undertakers will keep it. He told me many times that he wanted to give it to you when he was ready to go."

Ming could not believe his father had actually said that, but he said, "O.K.," then continued in Chinese, "We go now."

The young man in the office of the undertaker greeted them cordially. He listened politely while Ming explained that they had come for the gold watch that his father had been wearing when they had taken him away. The man said that he would check on it and glided into another office. He returned and said with a smile, "I'm sorry, but your father had no watch when he was brought in."

Ming interpreted for his mother. She looked sharply at the man and said to Ming, "He lies. Your father always wore watch. They try to steal it." Only the knowledge that his mother's eyes were filling with tears kept Ming from hurrying her out of the office. He turned to the man, who was listening curiously.

"My mother says that she is sure that he had it on," he said.

"I'm sorry," the man said with a shrug of his shoulders.

The condescension[13] on the man's face struck deep into Ming and his anger began to rise within him. Did this man think that he was talking to a child? He spoke deliberately, trying to keep the tremor out of his voice, "I suggest that you check on it again."

"But I'm sure it is not here."

Ming used his deepest tones to say, "If the watch isn't found we will go to the police."

A slight twitch passed over the man's face, but he recovered quickly and said, "Of course, we may have overlooked it. I'll check again." He disappeared into the

---

13. **condescension** (kahn-duh-SEN-shuhn) *n.* dealing with others in a scornful way, looking down on others

inner office. It was not long before he strode back in, waving his fist triumphantly.[14] "We did find it in a pocket we had overlooked," he said. He put the watch into Ming's outstretched hand.

Closing his fingers over the watch without looking at it, Ming muttered, "Thank you," and, taking his mother's arm, walked out.

Ming blinked at the sudden wintry sunlight. He stopped with his mother in the shadow of a building and looked at the watch in his hand. It was large and heavy, attached to a massive-looking chain. It must have been many years old for it was of the type whose face is protected by a snap cover. He squeezed down the stem and the cover flipped open. Inside the cover, he saw several words engraved in ornate[15] script. Squinting his eyes against the brightness he read, "For Ming, my son." His mouth was suddenly dry and he had difficulty swallowing as he tried to moisten it.

His mother was watching him. "Only last year, your father had something put in cover," she said.

Ming couldn't speak. They started walking homeward.

"You are number one son, head of family now, but after funeral, you must go back to Mrs. Warner and to school," his mother said.

"But the family—"

"Many things a woman can do at home to earn money."

"No," Ming said firmly, "I will work and go to night school."

His mother started to say something further, but Ming stopped her with, "Remember, I am number one son, head of family."

He took her arm to help her across the street.

---

14. **triumphantly** (treye-UM-fuhnt-lee) *adv.* successfully
15. **ornate** (awr-NAYT) *adj.* highly decorative

# *AFTER YOU READ*

## Exchanging Backgrounds and Cultures

1. Why does Ming feel resentful toward his father? What causes his attitude to change?
2. Why doesn't Ming console his mother?
3. What actions does Ming take at the end of the story that show he has accepted his role as the number one son?

## What Do You Think?

Which character or event in this story was most meaningful to you? Why was it special?

## Experiencing Fiction

At the end of the story, Ming assumes the responsibility of providing for his family. What difficulties do you think he might encounter as the family provider? Write a continuation of the story. Tell about an event or a sequence of events that takes place after Ming's father's funeral.

***Optional Activity*** Write a story about a character who experiences an internal conflict—a struggle that occurs within the character's mind. You may want to draw on a personal experience or on the experience of someone you know. For example, "Number One Son" is drawn from the author's painful loss of his own father.

# *INTRODUCTION*
## from Dragonwings

Laurence Yep was born in 1948 in San Francisco, California, and raised in a predominantly African American neighborhood. As a child, Yep would travel each day from his community to San Francisco's Chinatown, where he attended school. Yep recalls that it wasn't until he entered high school that he was exposed to mainstream culture. Challenged to write by a high school English teacher, Yep sold his first science fiction story when he was 18. Since then, he has written many books for young people. Two novels that reflect Yep's interest in science fiction are *Sweetwater* and *Dragon of the Lost Sea*. Yep considers his childhood experience of switching cultural environments to be the reason he became interested in science fiction and fantasy. These two types of literature interested Yep because they told stories of people who adapted to strange new worlds.

Aside from science fiction, Yep also writes stories that reflect his interest in his Chinese American heritage. The following excerpt is from Yep's novel *Dragonwings*. It tells the story of a young boy who leaves his home in China to join his father in America.

# from *Dragonwings*

By Laurence Yep

## 1 The Land of the Demons (February-March, 1903)

Ever since I can remember, I had wanted to know about the Land of the Golden Mountains, but my mother had never wanted to talk about it. All I knew was that a few months before I was born, my father had left our home in the Middle Kingdom, or *China*, as the white demons call it, and traveled over the sea to work in the demon land. There was plenty of money to be made among the demons, but it was also dangerous. My own grandfather had been lynched about thirty years before by a mob of white demons almost the moment he had set foot on their shores.

Mother usually said she was too busy to answer my questions. It was a fact that she was overworked, for Grandmother was too old to help her with the heavy work, and she had to try to do both her own work and Father's on our small farm. The rice had to be grown from seeds, and the seedlings transplanted to the paddies,[1] and the paddies tended and harvested. Besides this, she always had to keep one eye on our very active pig to keep him from rooting[2] in our small vegetable patch. She also had to

---

1. **paddies** (PAD-eez)  *n.* fields where rice is grown
2. **rooting** (ROOT-ihng)  *v.* digging or turning up the snout

watch our three chickens, who loved to wander away from our farm.

Any time I brought up the subject of Golden Mountain, Mother suddenly found something going wrong on our farm. Maybe some seedlings had not been planted into their underwater beds properly, or perhaps our pig was eating the wrong kind of garbage, or maybe one of our chickens was dirtying our doorway. She always had some good excuse for not talking about the Golden Mountain. I knew she was afraid of the place, because every chance we got, she would take me into the small temple in our village and we would pray for Father's safety, though she would never tell me what she was afraid of. It was a small satisfaction to her that our prayers had worked so far. Mother was never stingy about burning incense for Father.

I was curious about the Land of the Golden Mountain mainly because my father was there. I had, of course, never seen my father. And we could not go to live with him for two reasons. For one thing, the white demons would not let wives join their husbands on the Golden Mountain because they did not want us settling there permanently. And for another thing, our own clans discouraged wives from leaving because it would mean an end to the money the husbands sent home to their families—money which was then spent in the Middle Kingdom. The result was that the wives stayed in the villages, seeing their husbands every five years or so if they were lucky—though sometimes there were longer separations, as with Mother and Father.

We had heavy debts to pay off, including the cost of Father's ticket. And Mother and Grandmother had decided to invest the money Father sent to us in buying more land and livestock. At any rate, there was no money to spare for Father's visit back home. But my mother never complained about the hard work or the loneliness. As she said, we were the people of the Tang, by which she meant we were a tough, hardy, patient race. (We did not call ourselves *Chinese*, but the people of the Tang, after that famous dynasty that had helped settle our area some eleven hundred years ago. It would be the same as if an *English* demon called himself a man of the *Tudors*, the dynasty of *Henry VIII* and of *Elizabeth I*—though demon names sound so drab compared to ours.)

But sometimes Mother's patience wore thin. It usually happened when we walked over to the small side room in the Temple, where classes were also held. Like many other people, Mother and Grandmother could neither read nor write; but for a small fee, the village schoolmaster would read one of Father's weekly letters to us or write a letter at our dictation. In the evening after dinner, we would join the line of people who had a husband or brothers or sons overseas. There we would wait until it was our turn to go inside the Temple, and Mother would nervously turn the letter over and over again in her hands until Grandmother would tell her she was going to wear out the letter before we could read it.

To tell the truth, I knew as little about my father as I knew about the Land of the Golden Mountain. But Mother made sure that I knew at least one important thing about him: He was a maker of the most marvelous kites. Everyone in the village said he was a master of his craft, and his kites were often treasured by their owners like family heirlooms. As soon as I was big enough to hold the string, Mother took me out to the hill near our village where we could fly one of Father's kites. Just the two of us would go.

But you won't appreciate my father's skill if you think flying a kite—any kind of a kite—is just putting a bunch of paper on sticks up into the air. I remember the first time we went to fly a kite. There was nothing like the thrill when my kite first leaped up out of Mother's hands into the air. Then she showed me how to pull and tug and guide the kite into the winds. And when the winds caught the kite, it shot upward. She told me then how the string in my hand was like a leash and the kite was like a hound that I had sent hunting, to flush a sunbeam or a stray phoenix[3] out of the clouds.

But then she warned me that I had to stay alert, because sometimes the winds would try to tear the kite from my hand and I would have to hold on; or maybe the winds would try to drop my kite so it would smash to the ground. In that case, I would have to hurry up and reel in the slack and pull and steer the kite back into the winds until, just to get rid of the nuisance, the winds would take my kite where I wanted it to go.

I failed miserably the first times I tried to fly the kite, but Mother would not let me give up; and eventually I got quick enough and strong enough and smart enough so that my kite would be flying far overhead—so far away that I would lose sight of the string I had attached to the kite, and the kite would seem to be some colored patch of rainbow that was following me about. And then Mother would say that she was sure the kite was flying so high that the Jade Emperor, the Lord of Heaven and Earth, could admire my kite from his palace window. That was what flying a kite was all about.

And of course, Father's kites were the most truly balanced and the strongest and yet the most beautiful. In fact, his kites practically flew themselves. At first Mother only let me use Father's ordinary kites. He had made some special kites just before he left, when he knew my mother was pregnant; but Mother said I could not fly those kites

---

3. **phoenix** (FEE-nihks) *n.* a legendary, beautiful dark-red bird that lived 500 years, burned itself into ashes, then rose from the ashes to live again

until I was older and wiser—that is, when I turned eight. (The Tang people count the first nine months the mother carries the baby as the baby's first year. By demon reckoning, I was only seven.) I can't say who was prouder, my mother or I, when I finally managed to fly Father's special kites.

One was a sharply climbing swallow kite that was hard to get up, but there was nothing as fast as the swallow once it was up. The swallow swooped down with the slightest flick of the wrist or soared skyward with the tiniest jerk of the string. There was a large, long caterpillar kite, too, that took even longer to get up than the swallow, but once it was in the sky, it would stay forever, crawling back and forth over the clouds.

But the best thing about flying any of the kites was what it did for Mother. She would throw off all her cares and become young again, running with me or taking a turn at flying the kite. She would chatter on about the things that she and Father used to do when they were young, for they had both grown up here. She taught me everything that Father had ever shown her about flying kites. She said that one of the first things he would want to see when he returned home for a visit was how well I could fly them. But even at these moments, Mother would never speak of the Golden Mountain.

But I felt that since I was now eight and had mastered the hardest of Father's kites to fly, I was also old enough to get some answers. Mother still would not talk about the Golden Mountain, and in fact got mad at me. Grandmother felt sorry for me then, and she tried to tell me, among other things, why we called *America* the Land of the Golden Mountain. "It's because there's a big mountain there," she said. "The mountain's a thousand miles high and three thousand miles wide, and all a man has to do is wait until the sun warms the mountain and then scoop the gold into big buckets."

I squirmed on the bench. "Then why doesn't Father go get the gold instead of washing clothes?"

Grandmother shook her head. "It's because of the demons, you see. They roam the mountain up and down, and they beat up any of our men who try to get the gold. The demons use clubs as big as trees, and they kick them and do worse things. But if you do the work they tell you to do, then they let you take a little pinch of gold."

"Is that what happened to Grandfather? Did the demons catch him when he was trying to sneak some of the gold into his pockets?"

Grandmother sighed. She had been married to Grandfather only a year before he had left to make his fortune. "Perhaps, but," she added meaningfully, "the demons would just as soon beat up the Tang people for no good reason."

I nodded in understanding when Grandmother spoke of senseless beatings, for I had seen some of the other "guests" who had returned. There was Crook Arm, whose left arm dangled down uselessly by his side with two of his fingers missing. And there were other men whose backs were stooped, their fingers gnarled and their faces worn and tired as old masks (I did not know at the time that this was simply all from a life of hard work; I thought that torture had done this to them.) Many of them had the lung disease—*tuberculosis* was the demon word—and they hacked and spat constantly. Bit by bit they coughed up their broken lungs. Everyone in the village knew they had not long to live. Still more returned in their coffins, a silent testimony to the harshness of their demon "hosts."

I did not realize that I would find out at first hand about the Golden Mountain. One day, shortly after my ninth birthday (or eighth, as the demons count such things) we had a visitor, our cousin Hand Clap. He was in his fifties and lively as a cricket. He was a cousin because we had the same family name of Lee, though we had never seen him before. He said he had worked in the same store with my father and Uncle Bright Star overseas. Hand Clap obviously enjoyed the respect we gave him. Over tea, he told us he had decided to go back to the Land of the Golden Mountain and work a few more years while he still could. As he said, his two unmarried daughters were so ugly that they needed big dowries.[4] But we knew he was going back for another reason.

Things had not remained the same in the village as he remembered them. You would say something about a family or a village in the district, and he would say that was nothing and compare it to something bigger or better that he had seen in his youth. The silk was finer, the air cleaner, the rice sweeter, the fields more fertile, the girls prettier, the boys stronger when he was a young man. And then, too, when he spoke of his home life, he said there were too many women around and too much fussing. Though he had been married since he was sixteen, he had spent nearly thirty years of his marriage apart from his wife. On the other hand, his face lit up whenever he spoke of the good things about living on the Golden Mountain—for the Tang people had learned to have their own good times there.

Mother, of course, asked Hand Clap to take a small gift over to Father.

"I think I've come for a much bigger gift," he said, and handed us a letter from my father. "Make sure that it's your husband's hand," he said.

Mother nodded. Grandmother grunted that it was her son's writing all right. Then Hand Clap picked up the letter and began to read it.

In his letter, my father said that he and Uncle Bright

---

4. **dowries** (DOW-reez)  *n. pl.* the property that women bring to their husbands at marriage

Star thought it was time for me to cross the sea. I don't remember too much of what happened after that. I think that Mother said I was too young and Grandmother shouted that she had already lost a husband to the demons. Then her son had left her, and now she was about to lose her only grandson. Through all of this, Hand Clap sat unperturbed.

I sat bolt upright in my chair as Hand Clap spoke. "His father wants him to come over now with me. He'll learn the demon tongue better when he's young."

"But the demons will beat Moon Shadow," Mother protested.

"They don't do that so much anymore." Hand Clap carefully wiped his sticky fingers on his tunic sleeve. "And they wouldn't do it to a child. Even the demons have some principles."

Grandmother leaned forward on her cane. "And what if there are some lawless ones? They might not know any better and beat him."

"Not while I and the Company are around," Hand Clap said. "And there are always the fighting brotherhoods."

"Big talk," Grandmother grunted. "You're like the blind man who catches sparrows and calls them phoenixes."

"And besides," Mother insisted, "Shadow doesn't want to go yet."

It was an important moment in my life. Perhaps the most important. I had never seen my father, though I had often tried to picture him from Mother's and Grandmother's descriptions of him. His letters were certainly warm enough, filled with his worries about us and his longing to be back home. But a man cannot be a father in a letter.

Mother had talked quite a bit about him and so had Grandmother; but that too was not the same. They were speaking about a young man who had lived in the Middle Kingdom, not a man who had endured the hardships and loneliness of living in the demon land. I knew he made kites; but as marvelous as his kites were, he and I could not spend the rest of our lives flying kites. I was afraid of the Golden Mountain, and yet my father, who lived there, wanted me to join him. I only knew that there was a certain rightness in life—the feeling you got when you did something the way you knew you should. I owed it to Father to obey him in everything—even if it meant going to such a fearful place as the Golden Mountain. And really, how really frightening could it be if Hand Clap wanted to go back? I turned to Mother and Grandmother. "I want to go," I said.

And that was that. I won't go through the tearful goodbyes, or the boat ride on the river to Canton, the port city, or the first few days on the demon boat. I was young and I was homesick and I was frightened—especially of all the sailors, for they were so tall and big and hairy I thought that they were tiger demons—special tigers with magical powers. Perhaps I should explain here that the Tang word for demon can mean many kinds of supernatural beings. A demon can be the ghost of a dead person, but he can also be a supernatural creature who can use his great powers for good as well as for evil, just like the dragons. It is much trickier to deal with a demon of the Middle Kingdom than an *American devil*, because you always know that the *American devil* means you harm.

I was frightened, and Hand Clap did nothing to ease my fear. One fellow passenger remembered a story about demon sailors who had fattened up their Tang passengers. The Tang people had thought it was a good deal till they were marched off the boat into a butcher's shop. And then Hand Clap said that was nothing, and went on to talk about a ship of tiger demons who plied their trade between Canton and Hell, delivering the Tang men for work there. Hand Clap cared little about the truth, and loved to let his imagination run wild. He told us about how the sailors had slept upside down on top of their heads with knives between their teeth, and so on.

So I could not understand his excitement when we neared the land of the demons. To my disappointment, I only saw a brown smudge on the horizon—as the Middle Kingdom had looked from a distance. There was no glittering mound of gold to be seen. And then Hand Clap took me below to the hold to rehearse my story for the customs[5] demons. It was the one bit of practical advice I ever got from Hand Clap. When I came to the customs demons, I was to say I was eight, in the demon fashion, instead of nine as I truly was. I was to use my name in the wrong order, putting my family name after my personal name as the demons did. Otherwise the demons would write down the last word they heard, so that I would be called *Mister* Shadow instead of *Mister* Lee. If I made any of those mistakes, I might not be allowed to land as the son of my father.

There was reason to worry, too, for just a few years ago, the demons had broken their own laws and turned away over twenty thousand of their former guests who had expected to be readmitted. This figure does not even reflect the large number of Tang men who could not get into the country for the first time. The demons, it seemed, were determined to cut down on the number of Tang people living on the Golden Mountain.

The demons kept us locked inside a long, two-story warehouse for a week before it was our turn to be questioned. I don't like to think about it too much. We were kept on the bottom story, where we slept and ate off

---

**5. customs** (KUHS-tums) *n. pl.* the government agency in charge of collecting taxes on imported and exported goods

the floors. All the time, we smelled the sewage and the bilge of the bay—besides which there was no way to bathe there, so after the long boat voyage, we were rather a fragrant group on our own.

Finally, though, when the demons called me for questioning, I found they already had a big bunch of papers on my father. Inside it was the record of his first interview, which ran for some one hundred and fifty pages. They spent an hour looking at it and then asking me questions about my village and kinsmen. They tried to trip me up so they could prove I was not my father's son, but they did not succeed.

Finally even the demons had to admit that I was who I claimed to be. Then they made me strip naked and took my measurements and poked me all around, and they wrote down all that information on a sheet of paper so that if I ever left their country, no one could sneak back in my place. They put that sheet into a new bunch of papers, which were on me. They also added the notes of our interview to that pile.

I only got my first close look at the land of the Golden Mountain when Hand Clap and I were finally released and we stood together before the open doorway leading out of the warehouse where all the immigrants were taken. I saw plenty of hills, but not one golden one. And all the demon houses looked so strange. They were boxlike in shape, with no courtyards inside them, as if the demons hated fresh air but liked being shut up in something like a trunk. The houses had almost no ornamentation and were painted in dull colors—when they were painted at all. The little boxlike houses seemed so drab to me that I even felt sorry for the demons who lived in them, for they lived like prisoners without knowing they were in a prison.

Hand Clap had already sent word to Father by a friend who had been ahead of us in line and who had been released the day before, so we knew Father and the others

would be waiting. I saw all the Tang men standing at the
foot of the pier before the warehouse. I clutched my
wooden box to my chest. It was about the length of my arm
and about a third that in width; and it had a cunning metal
clasp with a ring at the end. I would hook my finger into
the ring and pull it up and the lid would open almost
noiselessly. This was for my valuables. I played with the
catch now nervously, studying the men.

They were all dressed alike, in either denim jackets or
the big, black loose cotton tunics that reached to their hips
and had wide, winglike sleeves. They also wore heavy blue
demon trousers of denim. Some of them wore the cotton
slipperlike shoes of the Tang men, while others wore
demon boots. They all wore demon hats, with the crowns
pushed up full and high and the brims down flat. I found
myself wondering which of them were really Tang men and
which might be demons in disguise.

Hand Clap waved toward one knot of men. "That's
Uncle Bright Star." Hand Clap pointed at a fat, old man. He
pointed out the rest of our Company. I heard him say that
they must not have brought the wagon because of the crowds
down here and the long wait for us. "And that tall man there,"
Hand Clap finished, looking at me, "that's your father."

I started to run. The others said hello as I went past
them but I ignored them. I held my box so tightly against
my chest that it hurt to breathe. Then I looked up at the
tall man who stood over me. He was nearly five foot eight,
which was tall for a Tang man in those days. He had a long,
sharp face with almost elfin eyes.

He was my father and yet he was a stranger to me. I
had never seen him.

I thought to myself, how can we ever speak to one
another? He's as strange to me as a demon.

And then my father smiled. "Hello, boy," he said. He
knelt down on the pier and held out his arms. "I've waited
a long time to do this. Too long."

And I dropped my box and ran into his arms. I had arrived.

## 2 The Company
## (April, 1903)

"So this is your boy," Uncle Bright Star said.

"Yes, Uncle." Father pushed me forward.

Uncle studied me as he would a new flatiron,[6] looking for flaws. I stared back at him. They don't make men like Uncle Bright Star anymore. His hands were calloused[7] by mining the *California* streams for gold, and his left index finger was twisted slightly from an accident when he had been helping to dig tunnels through the mountains for the railroad. Uncle had few "classmates" left. Classmates was the term which one government official might use for another official who had passed the government exams in the same year as he. But Uncle liked to say that the demons had examined him more rigorously than any government exam.

He was in his eighties and short and fat and built like a rock. He had a round face, with broad cheeks and a weak chin that made his thick lips seem to protrude even more. His belly stuck out above his pants top. It was usually covered by the loose tunic all the Tang men wore, but today he had worn a special blue silk coat.

"Don't you know it's impolite to stare, boy?" Uncle grunted.

"Why are you doing it then, sir?"

He rapped my forehead with his knuckle. "This boy

---

6. **flatiron** (FLAT-eye-uhrn) *n.* an iron for pressing clothes
7. **calloused** (KAL-uhst) *adj.* hard, thickened skin often caused by hard work

has character, at least." Everyone laughed, relieved. I had been accepted. Uncle turned to Father. "You're a lucky man, Windrider."

"Windrider?" I asked Father. "That's not your name."

"It is now," Father said. "I'll explain later."

It was a good thing that my father was with me. The thousands of miles I had crossed were nothing compared to the last mile or so between the docks and the town of the Tang people, *Chinatown*. I kept twisting my head this way and that to look at the hills until Father stopped. "What's the matter?" he asked.

"Which one is the Golden Mountain?"

Father did not even look at me, but turned around to look at poor Hand Clap. "Those two years in the Middle Kingdom haven't changed you one bit."

"Oh, now," Hand Clap mumbled. He scratched at his neck in embarrassment. "After all, the truth's what you make it."

Uncle Bright Star snorted. "It's a good thing you don't keep the books."

Father clapped his hand on my shoulder. "Boy, you have to realize that there was never a flea that Hand Clap didn't call a horse, and there was never a horse that he didn't call an elephant."

"And there has never been a country big enough to hold the elephant that Hand Clap has seen," Lefty laughed. He was bent almost double, hefting[8] my straw chest with his good hand as it rested on his back.

"You mean there's no Golden Mountain?" I was disappointed and felt a little betrayed.

"Not that we've ever seen." Uncle Bright Star added more kindly, "Though we've often wished it."

---

8. **hefting** (HEFT-ihng) *v.* lifting a heavy object

"Oh," I said in a very small voice.

Father took my hand kindly. "But there's a lot left to the demons' land that we haven't seen. Maybe we'll run across it yet."

"And like I've always said, that will be the day that everyone in the world decides to use copper and not gold for money," Uncle said.

"Then we'll look for a mountain of copper," Father laughed.

"And we'll let Hand Clap be our guide," added White Deer.

"And I'll guide you, cousins, straight and true," said Hand Clap, "for there's nothing I can't do. I can dig up a mountain, drink up a lake, outrun the wind. . . ." Hand Clap rambled on.

Father took the opportunity to whisper to me. "Stick close to me, Moon Shadow, and don't be afraid."

To get to the Tang people's town, you see, we had to pass through the *Barbary Coast*. . . . Walking up the street, I nearly lost heart. To me, the wooden houses seemed like shells of wood which terrible monsters had spun about themselves. It seemed as if the monsters would break out any moment through the wooden walls and grab me. One demon building in particular was very bad. . . .

A young white demon pushed through its doors. He was in strange clothes of black and white that were obviously dress-up. I wondered if he were some kind of special demon. I watched as he . . . quietly sat down.

His eyes crossed. *"What are you looking at, you little"*—it sounded like— *"chai-na-maan?"*

I looked at Father for a translation, but he had grown angry. Uncle Bright Star stepped in between us and bowed. *"No sabe. No sabe. So sorry."*

And the others gathered around us and began pushing us up the steep hill toward the safety of the town of the Tang people.

Suddenly, I felt as if I had come home. I can see the town of the Tang people even now in the late afternoon sun—not as it is now, full of souvenir shops and neon signs, but as it was then. The houses and the stores had all the right colors and shapes, for they had been built not by demons but by the Tang people. It looked much like the streets in Canton, the city in the Middle Kingdom from which I had sailed. The roofs of the buildings here were tiled and arched, and the walls, windows, and doorways were in gold or red or green. Before the fronts of the buildings were sensible safeguards against demons of any kind. There were lions lying down protectively before some; other houses had pictures of the door guardians on their doors, and still others had scrolls of red paper on the doorways, asking a certain god to protect the inhabitants[9] against demons.

On the blank walls of some buildings were long, narrow strips of red paper upon which words had been painted in thick, black ink. My father told me that some of them were advertisements, offering a heavy winter coat for sale, or somebody's services in writing a letter home, or perhaps a request to buy a demon watch. Above the posters and storefronts were balconies upon which men lounged, their faces turned toward the sun and their shadows arching behind them on the walls like long tails.

There was a breeze blowing down the hill and the men had gathered outside, standing on the sidewalks, their hands behind their backs, talking amiably.[10] In their dark tunics[11] and pants, they looked like shadows—a street of

---

**9. inhabitants** (ihn-HAB-ih-tuhnts) *n. pl.* people living in a dwelling
**10. amiably** (AY-mee-uh-blee) *adv.* in a friendly way
**11. tunics** (TOO-nihks) *n. pl.* long, loose blouses

shadows, flitting here and there, talking in high, loud, excited voices. (People who think the Tang people are quiet have never listened to us in our own homes, where the conversation is carried on at the level of a shout.) And from some room far above the street came the lonely, peaceful sound of a moon guitar.

The streets were narrow, and the tall, three-story buildings on either side made them seem even narrower. Vendors shuffled along in the dusty streets because the sidewalks were too crowded. Over their shoulders the vendors had heavy poles, from which they balanced baskets at either end—some with vegetables, others with pastries, or candies, or toys. Their loads seemed heavy enough until the demon wagons rolled toward them, pulled by the huge-bodied demon horses with their breaths blowing and the sweat glistening on their flanks. Then the vendors had to dodge nimbly to avoid being trampled under the heavy hooves, while the demon drivers shouted largely unintelligible curses at them.

There were groceries and herbal shops, clothing shops and laundries, halls that housed the brotherhoods or the district associations of the offices of family clans. Uncle pointed out the building of the district from which my family came and to which I could go for help. Besides that, there was the Lee family building, which would help everyone who was named Lee.

But most interesting to me were the men who sold their products from the stalls on the street. There was a butcher who worked in the mouth of a narrow alley. Behind the butcher were cages with fresh chickens waiting to be killed for the buyer, and before him was a big zinc washbasin filled with fresh fish. . . .

There were men in long narrow stalls set against the sides of buildings who sold toys and different candies—

one a type of sweet but hot-tasting, candied ginger[12] that was a bright orange-red in color. There were dried fruits that you could buy—sweet, semi-sweet, or salty. These you sucked inside your mouth till all the flavor was gone, and then you stripped the moistened meat away from the seed. There were apricot candies pressed flat into wafers; thin, white, curled strips of coconut candy; several kinds of disclike rice cookies; and so on. And in the doorways men sat on the stoops selling various newspapers gathered in piles around them. . . .

We stopped before a small, neat, three-story building painted bright red and green. On the front of the building was a huge sign on which were painted Tang people's symbols and demon words, announcing to the whole wide world that this was the Company of the Peach Orchard Vow. The demons always thought the name was funny. Uncle let them laugh. It was Uncle who told me that the Peach Orchard Vow was a famous vow, taken by the man who became the god of war and his two sworn brothers, to serve the people and help one another. On the door were painted the names of the two door guardians who kept the demons away. And on the windows were painted the words for Long Life and Prosperity.[13]

With a flourish, Uncle opened the front door for me and ushered me inside. "A superior home for superior men," he said. Uncle was fond of the phrase "the superior man," which he said he had taken from the wise man Confucius.[14]

I stepped in and looked around. The air inside smelled of soap and food and sweat. The bottom floor was given over to the laundry. The washing was done in the basement

---

12. **ginger** (JIHN-juhr)  *n.* a plant often used as a spice or perfume
13. **Prosperity** (prah-SPER-uh-tee)  *n.* good fortune or success
14. **Confucious** (kuhn-FYOO-shuhs) a Chinese philosopher and teacher

and in the back half of the first floor. A long curtain shut the back half off from view. In the front half, the half where I was now, there was a circular stove, with a broad rack on top, that stood in the middle of the floor. Spare flatirons heated up on the rack. When a man's iron cooled, he took another from the rack and put the cold one back on the rack to reheat. On the walls to either side of the stove and within reaching distance were ironing boards that folded down from the wall itself.

On the walls above the ironing boards were strips of thick, bright red paper with poems and sayings on them. Since the words of the Tang people were more alive— more like pictures, really—handwriting was more of an art form than among demons. All the poems and the sayings were done in lively, or lovely, hands. The most delicately written poem had been done by Lefty. . . . The poem went like this:

> Upon my bed
> Lies the bright moonlight
> Like frost upon the earth.
>
> Lifting my eyes,
> I see the bright moon.
> Closing my eyes,
> I see home.

The poem hung above Lefty's ironing board.

There were other, more conventional pious[15] sayings up on the walls. Ones like: "Peace and prosperity upon this store." They had been written by a man who had belonged to the Company before us. And there was one strip, faded and smoke-smudged by time, which had been written by one of the men who had founded the Company and who was long since dead. The founder had written: "The three

---

**15. pious** (PEYE-uhs) *adj.* showing religious devotion

virtues of the Stranger are to be silent, to be cunning, but above all to be invisible." Uncle told me that the warning had been taken from one of the Middle Kingdom's oldest books, "Classic of Changes."

All of us went up the stairs that led to the second floor. This was used as a kitchen and relaxation room, where the Company could read or gossip or play Mah-Jongg,[16] the game with tiles that is something like the demons' card game of *gin rummy*. On the third floor were our sleeping quarters. . . .

At sixty, White Deer was the second oldest in the Company. Technically speaking, White Deer, Uncle, and Hand Clap were all partners. (Hand Clap had originally sold his share of the laundry to the other two when he had returned home to the Middle Kingdom, but now that he had come back to the Land of the Golden Mountain, he had bought back his share). Lefty, Black Dog (Uncle's son), Father, and I only worked for wages till the day we could buy a junior partnership. But White Deer and Hand Clap never lorded it over any of us. We were all equally under Uncle's orders. . . .

---

**16. Mah-Jongg** (MAH-JAHNG) *n.* a game invented in China and played with tiles

# AFTER YOU READ

## Exchanging Backgrounds and Cultures

1. What does the narrator reveal about his attitude toward the United States and mainstream society?

2. Why is it important to the narrator to learn to fly his father's kites? What is the purpose of flying kites in Chinese culture?

3. Why does the narrator decide to go to the United States despite his fears? What does the narrator's decision suggest about traditional Chinese values?

## What Do You Think?

Which part of this excerpt was most interesting to you? Why was it meaningful?

## Experiencing Fiction

As you have just read, the narrator is united with his father who takes him to the Tang people's town. Think about what might happen next. What will be the narrator's impressions of his father, the Golden Mountain, the Company, and the "demons"? What adventures or hardships lie in store for him? Jot your ideas down on a piece of paper. Then continue the story where the second chapter of the novel leaves off. Focus the action on one of the ideas from your list.

**Optional Activity** Write a story about a place that you have visited. Like the narrator of *Dragonwings*, compare the actual place with your prior expectations of it. Remember to include descriptive details that focus on setting, the time and place of the action.

# UNIT 2: FOCUS ON WRITING

You can come up with a wealth of possible stories by drawing from your personal experiences and your imagination. If you develop a story about made-up characters and events—whether they are based on personal experiences or your imagination—you are creating a piece of fiction.

## Writing a Short Story

Short stories capture characters caught up in a single conflict. Write a short story that develops a conflict between characters.

## The Writing Process

Good writing requires both time and effort. An effective writer completes a number of stages that together make up the writing process. The stages of the writing process are given below to help guide you through your assignment.

### Prewriting

You can collect ideas for your short story in many ways. One way is to interview a classmate and ask each other questions about your interests. Another way is freewriting. Just write freely and rapidly. Then circle ideas that might make a good topic.

Once you have decided on a topic, you are ready to plan your story. Make a chart with a column for each of the five major elements in a story: setting, characters, conflict, plot, and theme. Brainstorm for ideas for each element, and place them in the appropriate column.

The following questions can help you to develop the various parts of your story before you begin to write.

**Setting:** Where does the story take place? During what year and season does the action occur?

**Characters:** Who will be the protaganist, or main

character? What other characters will take part in the action? How will you reveal the personality of each character? For example, in *Number One Son* the father's character is revealed through Ming's and other characters' recollections of him.

**Conflict:** What is the central conflict? Is it internal (within the character's mind) or external (between the character and some outside force)?

**Plot:** What events will take place? What event will spark the central conflict? What will be the high point, or climax, of the story? How will the conflict be resolved?

**Theme:** Will the story have a message for the reader? If so, how will that message be revealed?

Finally, consider how you will tell the story. Will one of the characters narrate the story? Or will you use a narrator who is not involved in the story?

### Drafting and Revising

Using your prewriting chart, begin drafting your story. As you draft, allow your thoughts to flow onto the paper. You will have a chance to revise your work later.

As you revise, make sure that you have developed your characters through dialogue and action and that the dialogue is realistic. Also be sure that you have created a clear picture of the setting. Finally, consider whether you have developed the plot in a way that will keep the reader's interest.

### Proofreading and Publishing

Once you have finished revising, carefully proofread your draft. Correct any errors in spelling, grammar, punctuation, and capitalization. Then make a neat final copy of your story.

Finally, consider how you will publish your story. You may want to read it aloud to your classmates, family, and friends. You may also want to submit it to a national magazine that publishes student writing.

# UNIT 3

# POETRY OF THE CHINESE AMERICANS

Poetry is a compact literary form. Most poets use a variety of literary devices, such as repetition, imagery, and figurative language, to express their thoughts.

**Repetition** is the repeated use of any element of language. Two important types of repetition are **alliteration**, the repetition of consonant sounds at the beginnings of words or accented syllables, and **parallelism**, the repetition of a grammatical structure.

**Imagery** refers to a poet's use of words to create mental pictures or images. An image may appeal to any one of the five senses, though in literature, visual images are the most common. For instance, in Cathy Song's poem "Lost Sister," the image of jade is associated with the speaker's longing for China.

**Figurative language** is language that uses figures of speech. A figure of speech is a way of saying one thing to mean another. Two figures of speech are **simile** and **metaphor**. A simile compares two dissimilar objects using *like* or *as*. In "A Soil With Rain And Sunshine," the simile "And those with integrity are as/leaf-stripped trees" compares proud Chinese Americans to bare trees. A metaphor is a comparison in which one thing is spoken of as though it were something else. For instance, Wing Tek Lum uses the metaphor of an apple peel for Chinese Americans in "Minority Poem."

The other poets in this unit also use these various techniques to bring their poems to life. In the first group of poems, the writers focus on family relationships to examine their connection to their heritage. The poets in the second group explore the dual identity of Chinese Americans. As you read each poem, pay careful attention to the literary devices each poet uses.

Untitled. *Asian American Arts Center*. Oil portrait by Pamela Chin Lee.

# INTRODUCTION

## Section 1:
## Relationships

Each poem in this group focuses on the relationship between the speaker of the poem and the speaker's family. The concept of family can be viewed symbolically as well as literally. A sister or grandfather may represent not only the speaker's actual relative, but also the struggles, values, and beliefs of the entire culture. Likewise, the relationships can be extended to include the speaker's connection to his or her cultural heritage, as well as to the immediate family.

In Alan Chong Lau's poem "a chinese landscape painting in california—18ç," the speaker creates a contrasting portrait of his family engaged in traditional Chinese rituals against the backdrop of the mountains of California. James Lim's poem "Grandfather" compares the speaker's aging grandfather to the old roots of a tree. This suggests that the grandfather represents the speaker's roots or cultural heritage. In "Lost Sister" by Cathy Song, the speaker explores her own connection to her cultural heritage through the struggles of both Chinese and Chinese American women. The last poem, "Eating Together" by Li-Young Lee, examines the way one Chinese American family keeps their father's memory alive by taking part in a traditional Chinese family meal.

# a chinese landscape painting in california—18?

by Alan Ching Lau

*for david izu, painter*

i see my family:
father washing bok choy in icy water
sits a straw hat on a rock

grandmother
a suspension of baskets defines the shoulders
red mud to reinforce a sluice[1]

mother chasing down a chicken
wields an object resemblng a cleaver
a lucky coin embedded at handle's end
catches a glint of sun

still asleep in long grass, a sister,
buds of flowers peek out of a tiny fist

overhead flocks of raucous birds
that don't speak our language
in fluent chinese i am yelling,
"papa, papa, what are those birds saying?"

---

**1. sluice** (SLOOS) *n.* an artificial channel or passage for water

not seen on the extreme right
a group of miners
coming to levy[2] taxes on our life
whiskey on their breath
curls the clouds

there is no gold
in these surrounding hills
but how were we to know?

in a lower righthand corner
under dense foliage
the artist leaves his name
in branches of blood

i read the caption
in the catalogue
looking for some explanation
and find:

"by now
the sierra
has eroded this all
to dust riding wind"

---

**2. levy**  (LEV-ee)  *v.* to collect (as in a tax)

# *Grandfather*

by James Lim

You sit cushioned from the world
in that chair;
you rest, and I watch.
The stillness of the room
settles lightly on the floor,
settles lightly like dust—
it streams
down to the earth,
is laden with sunlight.
You are old
like roots are old.
You have earthen eyes
made fertile with older days:
watery days without end, seemingly,
and days
with a stillness in the air
like a fog, thick and lonely.
You waited, always, for mountains,
but now you rest. The room is silent,
and you are old,
your roots are old,
Tell me a story
before the sun sets.

# Lost Sister

by Cathy Song

There is a sister
across the ocean,
who relinquished her name,
diluting jade green
with the blue of the Pacific.
Rising with a tide of locusts,
she swarmed with others
to inundate another shore.
In America,
there are many roads
and women can stride along with men.

But in another wilderness,
the possibilities,
the loneliness,
can strangulate like jungle vines.
The meager provisions and sentiments
of once belonging—
fermented roots, Mah-Jongg tiles and firecrackers—
set but a flimsy household
in a forest of nightless cities.
A giant snake rattles above,
spewing black clouds into your kitchen.
Dough-faced landlords
slip in and out of your keyholes,
making claims you don't understand,
tapping into your communication systems
of laundry lines and restaurant chains.

You find you need China:
your one fragile identification,
a jade link
handcuffed to your wrist.
You remember your mother
who walked for centuries,
footless—
and like her,
you have left no footprints,
but only because
there is an ocean in between,
the unremitting space of your rebellion.


# *Eating Together*

## by Li-Young Lee

In the steamer is the trout
seasoned with slivers of ginger,
two sprigs of green onion, and sesame oil.
We shall eat it with rice for lunch,
brothers, sister, my mother who will
taste the sweetest meat of the head,
holding it between her fingers
deftly, the way my father did
weeks ago. Then he lay down
to sleep like a snow-covered road
winding through pines older than him,
without any travelers, and lonely for no one.

# AFTER YOU READ

## Exchanging Backgrounds and Cultures

1. What do "Lost Sister" and "a chinese landscape painting in california—18?" reveal about the experiences of Chinese Americans when they first immigrated to the United States?

2. In "Grandfather" and "a chinese landscape painting in california—18?," how do the speakers express their connection to their heritage through their portrayal of family members?

3. In "Eating Together," how do the family members feel connected with the father?

## What Do You Think?

Which poem or poems in this group did you find especially meaningful? Why were they special?

## Experiencing Poetry

The poems in this section focus on family relationships. Think about your own family relationships. Do you have one relative who is especially important to you? What makes that relationship special? Write a poem about your relationship with that family member. Be sure to use concrete images to convey a vivid portrait of the person.

*Optional Activity* Write a poem that uses a metaphor to express your connection to home. Remember that a metaphor is a figure of speech in which one thing is spoken of as though it were something else. For instance, in Cathy Song's poem, she uses jade as a metaphor for her longings for China.

# *INTRODUCTION*

## Section 2: Identity

The poets represented in this section explore the differences between Chinese culture and U.S. culture and examine their own feelings about being caught between the two. In each case, the speaker tries to retain his or her traditional heritage while becoming a part of U.S. society. The speaker often experiences disappointment, confusion, and frustration during this process of self-discovery.

In "A Soil With Rain And Sunshine," Ling Chung explores the conflicting feelings of joy and disillusionment immigrants often experience in coming to the United States. The next poem, "Chinatown #1" by Laureen Mar, contrasts two generations of Chinese Americans. One preserves the customs of its traditional heritage, and the other adopts the language and values of the new land. In "Minority Poem," Wing Tek Lum exposes the prejudice many Chinese Americans face. The speaker feels left out or left over, treated like an outsider in his own country. Finally, in "Saying Yes" by Diana Chang, the speaker embraces her Chinese American identity.

# A Soil With Rain And Sunshine

by Ling Chung

I dreamt of a soil with rain
    and sunshine
Where men were tall and walked
    straight under the sky.

When I came close to you,
    America,
Your colorful spectrum dizzied
    my sight,
Your electronic momentum
    fused into
An immense metallic laughter.

In the whirling snow of my
    life's first winter
I listened attentively to your
    core . . .
Nothing came but silence.

Very few, including the long
    and the short-haired,
Comprehend that behind the
    glamour of
The world's first citizens
Are lives of quiet desperation.
Dreams of the pure, the free,
    and the beautiful,
Fade into space like jet trails

And those with integrity are as
    leaf-stripped trees
Standing on a barren horizon,
    torn by the wintry blasts.

# *Chinatown* #1

by Laureen Mar

She boards the bus at Chinatown,
holding the brown paper shopping bag
with twine handles that comes from
San Francisco or Vancouver.
It is worn thin with creases.
An oil spot darkens one side
where juice dripped from a warm
roast duck, another shopping trip.
Today there is fresh bok choy
wrapped in Chinese newspapers.
Grasping the rail with her right hand,
she climbs the steps carefully,
smiling at the driver, looking down
to check her footing, glancing
at him again. She sways down the aisle
as if she still carried wood buckets
on a bamboo pole through the village,
from the well to her house.
Her gray silk pajamas are loose,
better than "pantsuits."
Sometimes there are two or three women,
chattering with the quick, sharp tongue
of the wren: dried mushrooms too
expensive, thirteen dollars a pound now.
She sits down and sets the bag between her knees.
Her shoulder is close to mine.
I want to touch it, tell her I can understand
Chinese. Instead, I stare at the silver
bar crossing her back, and hope she knows
this is an Express; it does not stop before Genesee.

# *Minority Poem*

## by Wing Tek Lum

*For George Lee*

Why
we're just as American
as apple pie—
that is, if you count
the leftover peelings
lying on the kitchen counter
which the cook has forgotten about
or doesn't know
quite what to do with
except hope that the maid
when she cleans off the chopping block
will chuck them away
into a garbage can she'll take out
on leaving for the night.

# *Saying Yes*

by Diana Chang

"Are you Chinese?"
"Yes."

"American?"
"Yes."

"*Really* Chinese?"
"No . . . not quite."

"*Really* American?"
"Well, actually, you see . . ."

But I would rather say
yes

Not neither-nor,
not maybe,
but both, and not only

The homes I've had,
the ways I am

I'd rather say it
twice,
yes

# AFTER YOU READ

## Exchanging Backgrounds and Cultures

1. What do the speakers of "Minority Poem" and "Saying Yes" reveal about their sense of identity as Chinese Americans?

2. How do "A Soil With Rain And Sunshine" and "Minority Poem" express a sense of disillusionment with life in the United States?

3. How does "Chinatown #1" convey the contrast between two generations of Chinese Americans?

## What Do You Think?

Which poem or poems in this group especially interested you? How did the language, tone, and imagery affect you?

## Experiencing Poetry

The conflict between their Chinese heritage and their lives in the United States leaves the speakers of these poems struggling with their sense of identity. How would you describe your own cultural identity? What struggles have you experienced in discovering this identity? Write a poem about a personal struggle related to your sense of identity.

*Optional Activity* Write a poem that expresses your ideas about the United States. In your poem, use alliteration to create a musical effect and emphasize your main ideas. As you have read, alliteration is the repetition of consonant sounds at the beginnings of words or accented syllables. For instance, the "n" sound is repeated in the following lines from Diana Chang's "Saying Yes": "Not neither-nor,/ not maybe,/ but both, and not only."

# UNIT 3: FOCUS ON WRITING

Through vivid imagery and figurative language, poems can convey meaning and evoke emotion. Poems can also have a musical quality that is created through rhythm, rhyme, and other sound devices.

## Writing a Poem

Consider the following topics: an interesting person, a special place, a favorite activity. Then, write a poem about one of these topics or another topic of your choice.

## The Writing Process

Good writing requires both time and effort. An effective writer completes a number of stages that together make up the writing process. The stages of the writing process are given below to help guide you through your assignment.

### Prewriting

After you have decided on a topic, you can use a technique called five-senses cuing to develop concrete images related to your topic. Begin by jotting down as many images as you can that appeal to the sense of sight. Then repeat this process with the other four senses: hearing, touch, smell, and taste. When you have finished, underline the most powerful images.

Next, think about the theme, or central message, that you would like to express in your poem. The theme should grow out of the imagery and events you plan to include in the poem, as well as your own feelings and personal experiences.

Then think about the tone, or the attitude toward your subject, that you want to convey. Should the tone of your poem be serious, funny, happy, sad, anxious, tranquil? For instance, the sad, regretful tone of Ling Chung's poem "A Soil With Rain And Sunshine" captures the speaker's disappointment with America.

Finally, think about the form of your poem and your use of rhythm and sound devices. Where will the lines end? How many stanzas will there be? Will you use a regular rhythm, or pattern of accented syllables? Will you use rhyme? Will you use other sound devices?

### Drafting and Revising

Using your lists of images, begin drafting your poem. As you draft, focus on using concrete details to express your ideas. You should also consider how your poem sounds. After every few lines, you may want to read your poem aloud to yourself. Does it have the type of rhythm you intended?

When you have finished drafting, put your poem aside for a while. Then look at it with a fresh eye. Note any lines or words that do not sound right or convey the meaning you intended. Think about the following questions: Could any of the images be improved? Are any of the words or images unnecessary? Are you satisfied with the poem's rhythm? Could you improve your poem by using more sound devices? After you have finished reviewing your poem, make appropriate revisions. You may then want to read your poem aloud again and make additional revisions.

Finally, choose an appropriate title for the poem. The title can reflect the subject of the poem, or it can add to the poem's mystery!

### Proofreading and Publishing

Now proofread your poem for any errors in spelling, grammar, punctuation, and capitalization. In poetry, it is acceptable to use unconventional punctuation and capitalization. For example, in "a chinese landscape painting in california—18?," Lau does not use capitali-zation at all.

Poetry is especially effective when read aloud. Hold a poetry reading in your class. You might also want to create a classroom collection that includes the poems and illustrations of your classmates.

# UNIT 4

# DRAMA OF THE CHINESE AMERICANS

**Drama** is literature that is meant to be performed. It can be presented live in front of an audience, or captured on film and shown on television or in the movies. When you read a drama, you should try to imagine how it would appear on the stage or screen.

Like novels and short stories, dramas contain plots, conflicts, settings, and characters. Dramas generally convey one or more themes.

The elements that make up a drama are dialogue and stage directions. Dialogue is the lines that the characters speak. Stage directions are the playwright's instructions to the director and actors. They indicate how the actors should speak and move; how the stage should look; and what movable pieces, or props, should be used by the actors. Stage directions also tell what kind of lighting and sound effects should be used during the performance.

Dramas are usually divided into sections, much as a novel is divided into chapters. The major divisions in a drama are called acts. Within an act, there are usually minor divisions called scenes. The excerpt you are about to read is the first act of David Henry Hwang's two-act drama *Family Devotions.*

In this act, Hwang presents three generations of a Chinese American family gathered in a modern California home. Hwang contrasts the traditional Chinese values and beliefs of the two grandmothers with the typical "American" attitudes and activities of the younger family members. As you read this act, try to imagine how the setting and characters look and how the events unfold onstage.

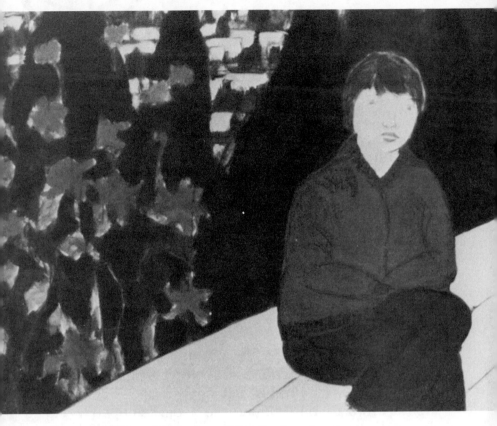

**In Front of Christmas Blossoms.** *Asian American Arts Center.*
Painting by Tsai-Tung Chang.

# *INTRODUCTION*
## from Family Devotions

David Henry Hwang, the son of Chinese immigrants, is a well-known and critically acclaimed playwright. His drama *M. Butterfly*, which opened on Broadway in 1988, won the Tony Award as best play of the year. Perhaps Hwang's greatest accomplishment as a playwright, however, lies in his ability to capture onstage the complexities of the Chinese American experience. Hwang strongly believes that "by confronting our ethnicity, we are simply confronting the roots of our humanity."

The act you are going to read is from a drama called *Family Devotions*. In this drama, the members of the family represent several generations of Chinese Americans. As such, their values and beliefs differ greatly. The youngest generation, raised in Southern California, cares little about the traditional ways of their grandmothers, who were born in China. These older women attempt to preserve their cultural and family history. The interaction between the characters reveals the importance of accepting one's own cultural identity, as well as that of others.

# from *Family Devotions*

## by David Henry Hwang

## *CHARACTERS*

JOANNE, late thirties, Chinese American raised in the
Philippines.

WILBUR, her husband, Japanese American, nisei (second
generation).

JENNY, their daughter, seventeen.

AMA, Joanne's mother, born in China, emigrated to the
Philippines, then to America.

POPO, Ama's younger sister.

HANNAH, Popo's daughter and Joanne's cousin, slightly
older than Joanne.

ROBERT, Hannah's husband, Chinese American, first
generation.

DI-GOU, Ama and Popo's younger brother, born and raised
in China, still a resident of the People's Republic of
China (P.R.C.).

CHESTER, Hannah and Robert's son, early twenties.

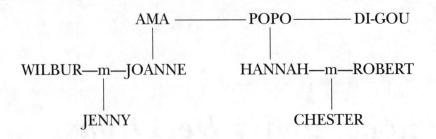

## SYNOPSIS OF SCENES

ACT I. Late afternoon, the lanai/sunroom and tennis court of a home in Bel Air, California.

## Act I

*T**he sunroom and backyard of a home in Bel Air. Everywhere is glass—glass roof, glass walls. Upstage of the lanai/sunroom is a patio with a barbecue and a tennis court. The tennis court leads offstage. As the curtain rises, we see a single spotlight on an old Chinese face and hear Chinese music or chanting. Suddenly, the music becomes modern-day funk or rock'n'roll, and the lights come up to reveal the set.*

*The face is that of DI-GOU, an older Chinese man wearing a blue suit and carrying an old suitcase. He is peering into the sunroom from the tennis court, through the glass walls. Behind him, a stream of black smoke is coming from the barbecue.*

*(Offstage)* Wilbur! Wilbur!

*(DI-GOU exits off the tennis court. Enter JOANNE, from the house. She is a Chinese American woman, attractive, in her mid-thirties. She sees the smoke coming from the barbecue.)*

JOANNE: Aiii-ya! *(She heads for the barbecue, and on her way notices that the sunroom is a mess.)* Jenny! *(She runs out to the barbecue, opens it up. Billows of black smoke continue to pour out.)* Oh, gosh. Oh, golly. *(To offstage)* Wilbur! *(She begins pulling burnt objects out of the barbecue.)* Sheee! *(She pulls out a chicken, dumps it onto the ground.)* Wilbur! *(She pulls out another chicken, does the same)* Wilbur, the heat was too high on the barbecue! *(She begins pulling out burnt objects and tossing them all over the tennis court.)* You should have been watching it! It could have exploded! We could all have been blown up! *(She picks up another chicken, examines it)* You think we can have some of this? *(She pauses, tosses it onto the court)* We'll get some more chickens. We'll put barbecue sauce on them and stick them into the microwave. *(She exits into the house holding a chicken on the end of her fork.)* Is this okay, do you think?

*(WILBUR appears on the tennis court. He is a Japanese American man, nisei, in his late thirties. His hair is permed. He wears tennis clothes.)*

WILBUR: Hon? *(He looks around.)* What's up? *(He picks a burnt chicken off the tennis court.)* Hon? *(He walks over to the barbecue.)* Who—? Why's the heat off? *(He walks around the tennis court picking up chickens.)* . . . *(He smears grease on his white tennis shirt, notices it)* . . . *(He dumps all the chickens except one, which he has forgotten to pick up, back into the barbecue. He walks into the sunroom, gets some ice, and tries to dab the stain.)* Hon? Will you come here a sec? *(He exits into the house.)*

*(JENNY appears on the tennis court. She is seventeen, WILBUR and JOANNE's daughter. She carries a large wire-mesh box.)*

JENNY: Chickie! *(Looking around)* Chickie? Chickie, where . . . did you go? You know, it's embarrassing. It's embarrassing being this old and still having to chase a chicken all over the house. *(She sees the one burnt chicken on the court. She creeps over slowly, then picks it up.)* Blaagh! Who cooked this? See, Chickie, this is what happens— what happens when you're a bad chickie.

*(CHESTER, a young Chinese American male in his early*

*twenties, appears on the tennis court. He tries to sneak up on* JENNY.)

JENNY: *(To chicken)* Look, if you bother Popo and Ama, I'm gonna catch . . . and you know what that means for you—chicken soccer. You'll be sorry. (CHESTER *is right behind* JENNY.) You'll be sorry if you mess with me. *(She turns around, catching* CHESTER.) Oh, good. You have to be here, too.

CHESTER: No, I don't. I've gotta pack.

JENNY: They'll expect you to be here when that Chinese guy gets here. What's his name? Dar-gwo?

CHESTER: I dunno. Dah-gim?

JENNY: Doo-goo? Something.

CHESTER: Yeah. I'm not staying.

JENNY: So what else is new?

CHESTER: I don't have time.

JENNY: You luck out 'cause you don't live here. Me— there's no way I can get away. When you leaving?

CHESTER: Tomorrow.

JENNY: Tomorrow? And you're not packed?

CHESTER: Don't rub it in. Listen, you still have my green suitcase?

JENNY: Yeah. I wish *I* had an excuse not to be here. All I need is to meet another old relative. Another goon.

CHESTER: Yeah. Where's my suitcase?

JENNY: First you have to help me find Chickie.

CHESTER: . . . !

AMA: *(Offstage)* Joanne!

CHESTER: *(To* JENNY) All right. I don't want them to know I'm here.

(CHESTER *and* JENNY *exit.* POPO *and* AMA *enter. They are* JOANNE'S *aunt and mother, respectively.)*

AMA: Joanne! Joanne! Jenny! Where is Joanne?

POPO: Probably busy.

AMA: Where is Jenny? Joanne?

POPO: Perhaps you can find, ah, Wilbur.

AMA: Joanne!

POPO: Ah, you never wish to see Wilbur.

AMA: I see him at wedding. That is enough. He was not at church again today.

POPO: Ah?

AMA: He will be bad influence when Di-gou arrive. Wilbur—holy spirit is not in him.

POPO: Not matter. He can perhaps eat in kitchen.

AMA: Outside!

POPO: This is his house.

AMA: All heart must join as one—

POPO: He may eat inside!

AMA: —only then, miracles can take place.

POPO: But in kitchen.

AMA: Wilbur—he never like family devotions.

POPO: Wilbur does not come from Christian family.

AMA: He come from Japanese family.

POPO: I mean to say, we—ah—very fortunate. Mama teach us all Christianity. Not like Wilbur family.

AMA: When Di-gou arrive, we will remind him. What Mama tells us.

POPO: Di-gou can remember himself.

AMA: No.

POPO: But we remember.

AMA: You forget—Di-gou, he lives in China.

POPO: So?

AMA: Torture. Communists. Make him work in rice fields.

POPO: I no longer think so.

AMA: In rice field, all the people wear wires in their heads— yes! Wires force them work all day and sing Communist song. Like this! *(She mimes harvesting rice and singing.)*

POPO: No such thing!

AMA: Yes! You remember Twa-Ling? Before we leave China, before Communist come, she say, "I will send you a picture. If Communists are good, I will stand—if bad, I will sit."

POPO: That does not mean anything!

AMA: In picture she sent, she was lying down!

POPO: Picture was not sent for ten years. Probably she forget.

AMA: You wait till Di-gou arrive. You will see.

POPO: See what?

AMA: Brainwash! You watch for little bit of wires in his hair.

(POPO *notices the lone burnt chicken on the tennis court.*)

POPO: What's there?

AMA: Where?

POPO: There—on cement.

AMA: Cannot see well.

POPO: There. Black.

AMA: Oh. I see.

POPO: Looks like *gao sai.*

AMA: They sometimes have problem with the dog.

POPO: Ha!

AMA: Very bad dog.

POPO: At home, dog do that?—we shoot him.

AMA: Should be punish.

POPO: Shot! *(Pause)* That no *gao sai.*

AMA: No? What then?

POPO: I don't know.

AMA: Oh, I know.

POPO: What?

AMA: That is Chickie.

POPO: No. That no Chickie.

AMA: They have a chicken—"Chickie."

*(They get up, head toward the chicken)*

POPO: No. That one, does not move.

AMA: Maybe sick. *(They reach the chicken.)* Aiii-ya! What happened to Chickie!

POPO: *(Picking it up)* This chicken very sick! *(She laughs.)*

AMA: Wilbur.

POPO: Huh?

AMA: Wilbur—his temper is very bad.

POPO: No!

AMA: Yes. Perhaps Chickie bother him too much.

POPO: No—this is only a chicken.

AMA: "Chickie" *is* chicken!

POPO: No—this—another chicken.

AMA: How you know?

POPO: No matter now. Like this, all chicken look same. Here. Throw away. No good.

AMA: Very bad temper. Japanese man. *(AMA sees POPO looking for a trash can.)* Wait.

POPO: Huh?

AMA: Jenny—might want to keep it.

POPO: This?

AMA: Leave here until we know. *(She takes the chicken from POPO.)*

POPO: No, throw away. *(She takes it back.)* Stink up whole place soon.

AMA: Don't want to anger Wilbur!

POPO: You pig-head!

AMA: He do this to Chickie—think what he will do to us?

POPO: *Zin gao tza!* [Always so much trouble!]

AMA: You don't know Japanese man!

   *(AMA knocks the chicken from POPO's hands; they circle around it like boxers sparring.)*

POPO: *Pah-di!* [Spank you!]

AMA: Remember? During war? Pictures they show us? Always—Japanese man kill Chinese!

POPO: Go away, pig-head!

AMA: In picture—Japanese always kill and laugh, kill and laugh.

POPO: If dirty, should throw away!

AMA: Sometimes—torture and laugh, too.

POPO: Wilbur not like that! Hardly even laugh!

AMA: When he kill Chickie, then he laugh!

*(They both grab the chicken;* JOANNE *enters, sees them)*

JOANNE: Hi, Mom, Auntie. Who cleaned up the chicken?

AMA: Huh? This is not Chickie?

POPO: *(To AMA)* Tell you things, you never listen. *Gong-gong-ah!* [Idiot!]

JOANNE: When's Hannah getting here?

POPO: Hannah—she is at airport.

JOANNE: We had a little accident and I need help programming the microwave. Last time, I put a roast inside and it disintegrated. She should be here already.

AMA: Joanne, you prepare for family devotions?

JOANNE: Of course, Mom. I had the maid set up everything just like you said.

*(She exits.)*

AMA: Good. Praise to God will bring Di-gou back to family. Make him rid of Communist demon.

POPO: He will speak in tongue of fire. Like he does when he is a little boy with See-goh-poh.

*(WILBUR enters the tennis court with an empty laundry basket. He heads for the barbecue. JOANNE follows him.)*

JOANNE: *(To WILBUR)* Hon, what are you going to do with those?

WILBUR: *(Referring to the burnt chicken)* I'm just going to give them to Grizzly. *(He piles the chickens into the basket.)*

JOANNE: All right. *(She notices that the mess in the lanai has not been touched.)* Jenny! *(To WILBUR)* But be careful not to give Grizzly any bones!

*(JOANNE exits.)*

WILBUR: *(To AMA and POPO)* How you doin', Mom, Auntie?

AMA: *(To* POPO, *sotto voce)*[1] Kill and laugh.

WILBUR: Joanne tells me you're pretty excited about your brother's arrival—pretty understandable, after all these years—what's his name again? Di-ger, Di-gow, something . . .

AMA: Di-gou!

WILBUR: Yeah, right. Gotta remember that. Be pretty embarrassing if I said the wrong name. Di-gou.

POPO: Di-gou is not his name.

WILBUR: What? Not his—? What is it again? Di-gow? De—?

AMA: Di-gou!

WILBUR: Di-gou.

POPO: That is not his name.

WILBUR: Oh. It's the tones in Chinese, isn't it? I'm saying the wrong tone: Di-gou? Or Di-gou? Or—

POPO: Di-gou meaning is "second brother."

WILBUR: Oh, I see. It's not his name. Boy, do I feel ignorant in these situations. If only there were some way I could make sure I don't embarrass myself tonight.

AMA: Eat outside.

WILBUR: Outside?

POPO: Or in kitchen.

WILBUR: In the kitchen? That's great! You two are real jokers, you know?

AMA: No. We are not.

WILBUR: C'mon. I should bring you down to the club someday. The guys never believe it when I tell them how much I love you two.

AMA: *(To* POPO*)* Gao sai.

(JENNY *enters the sunroom.*)

WILBUR: Right. *"Gao sai"* to you, too. *(He starts to leave, sees*

---

1. **sotto voce** (SAWT-aw VAW-che) an Italian expression, *in a soft voice*

JENNY) Wash your hands before you play with your grandmother.

JENNY: *(To* WILBUR) Okay, Dad. *(To* AMA) Do I have to, Ama?

AMA: No. Of course not.

JENNY: Can I ask you something personal?

AMA: Of course.

JENNY: Did Daddy just call you "dog . . ."?

AMA: Jenny!

POPO: Yes. Very good!

JENNY: Doesn't that bother you?

POPO: *(To* AMA) Her Chinese is improving!

JENNY: We learned it in Chinese school.

AMA: Jenny, you should not use this American word.

JENNY: Sorry. It just slipped out.

AMA: You do not use such word at school, no?

JENNY: Oh, no. Of course not.

AMA: You should not use anyplace.

JENNY: Right.

POPO: Otherwise—no good man wants marry you.

JENNY: You mean no rich man.

AMA: No—money is not important.

POPO: As long as he is good man.

*(Pause)*

AMA: Christian.

POPO: Chinese.

AMA: Good education.

POPO: Good school.

AMA: Princeton.

POPO: Harvard.

AMA: Doctor.

POPO: Surgeon.

AMA: Brain surgeon.

POPO: Surgeon general.

AMA: Otherwise—you marry anyone that you like.

JENNY: Ama, Popo—look, I'm only seventeen.

POPO: True. But you can develop the good habits now.

JENNY: I don't want to get married till I'm at least thirty or something.

POPO: By that time we are dead!

AMA: Gone to see God!

POPO: Lie in ground, arms cross!

JENNY: Look at it this way: how can I be a good mother if I have to follow my career around?

AMA: Your career will not require this.

JENNY: Yeah, it will. What if I have to go on tour?

AMA: Dental technicians do not tour.

JENNY: Ama!

POPO: Only tour—one mouth to next mouth: "Hello. Clean your teeth?"

JENNY: Look, I'm telling you, I'm going to be a dancer.

AMA: We say—you can do both. Combine skills.

JENNY: That's ridiculous.

POPO: Be first dancing dental technician.

JENNY: I don't wanna be a dental technician!

POPO: Dancing dental technician very rare. You will be very popular.

JENNY: Why can't I be like Chester?

AMA: You cannot be like Chester.

JENNY: Why not?

POPO: You do not play violin. Chester does not dance. No hope.

JENNY: I know, but, I mean, he's a musician. Why can't I be a dancer?

AMA: Chester—his work very dangerous.

JENNY: Dangerous?

AMA: He just receive new job—play with Boston Symphony.

JENNY: Yeah. I know. He's leaving tomorrow. So? What's so bad about Boston?

AMA: Conductor—Ozawa—he is Japanese.

JENNY: Oh, no. Not this again.

AMA: Very strict. If musicians miss one note, they must kill themself!

JENNY: Don't be ridiculous. That's no reason why I can't be like Chester.

POPO: But Chester—he makes plenty money.

JENNY: Yeah. Right. Now. But he has to leave home to do it, see? I want a career, too. So what if I never get married?

AMA: Jenny! You must remember—you come from family of See-goh-poh. She was a great evangelist.[2]

JENNY: I know about See-goh-poh. She was your aunt.

AMA: First in family to become Christian.

POPO: She make this family chosen by God.

JENNY: To do what? Clean teeth?

AMA: Jenny!

JENNY: Look, See-goh-poh never got married because of her work, right?

AMA: See-goh-poh was marry to God.

POPO: When Di-gou arrive, he will tell you his testimony. How See-goh-poh change his life.

AMA: Before, he is like you. *(To POPO)* You remember?

POPO: Yes. He is always so fussy.

JENNY: I'm not fussy.

AMA: Stubborn.

POPO: Complain this, complain that.

JENNY: I'm not complaining!

AMA: He will be very happy to meet you. Someone to complain with.

JENNY: I'm just telling you, there's no such thing as a dancing dental technician!

AMA: Good. You will be new discovery.

---

2. **evangelist** (ee-VAN-juh-lihst)  *n.* a traveling preacher

POPO: When Di-gou is a little boy, he never play with other children. He only read the books. Read books—and play tricks.

AMA: He is very naughty.

POPO: He tell other children there are ghosts hide inside the tree, behind the bush, in the bathroom at night.

AMA: One day, he feed snail poison to gardener.

POPO: Then, when he turns eight year old, See-goh-poh decide she will bring him on her evangilism tour. When he return, he has the tongue of fire.

JENNY: Oh, c'mon—those kind of things only happened in China.

AMA: No—they can happen here as well.

POPO: Di-gou at eight, he goes with See-goh-poh on her first evangelism tour—they travel all around Fukien[3]—thirty day and night, preach to all villages. Five hundred people accept Christ on these thirty day, and See-goh-poh heal many sick, restore ear to deaf, put tongue in mouth of dumb, all these thing and cast out the demon. Perhaps even one dead man—dead and wither—he rise up from his sleep. Di-gou see all this while carry See-goh-poh's bag and bring her food, ah? After thirty day, they return home. We have large banquet—perhaps twelve different dish that night—outside—underneath—ah—cloth. After we eat, See-goh-poh say, "Now is time for Family Devotions, and this time, he will lead." See-goh-poh point to Di-gou, who is still a boy, but he walk up in front of table and begin to talk and flame begin to come from his mouth, over his head. Fire. Fire, all around. His voice—so loud—praise and testify the miracle of God. Louder and louder, more and more fire, till entire sky fill with light, does not seem to be night, like middle of day, like twelve

---

8. **Fukien** (FOO-KYEN) *n.* province in Southeast China

noon. When he finish talk, sun has already rise, and cloth over our head, it is all burn, gone, ashes blow away.

*(JOANNE enters, pulling CHESTER behind. He carries a suitcase.)*

JOANNE: Look who's here!

POPO: Chester—good you decide to come.

JOANNE: He looked lost. This house isn't that big, you know.

*(Exits)*

AMA: *(To CHESTER)* You come for reunion with Di-gou. Very good.

CHESTER: Uh—look, I really can't stay. I have to finish packing.

AMA: You must stay—see Di-gou!

CHESTER: But I'm leaving tomorrow.

*(Doorbell)*

CHESTER: Oh, no.

JOANNE: Can someone get that?

JENNY: Too late!                                    *(Simultaneously)*

POPO: Di-gou!

AMA: *(To CHESTER)* You must! This will be Di-gou!

*(WILBUR crosses with basket, now full of chicken bones.)*

WILBUR: I'll get it. Chester, good to see you made it.

*(Exits)*

JENNY: He almost didn't.

CHESTER: I'm really short on time. I gotta go. I'll see you tomorrow at the airport.

POPO: Chester! When Di-gou arrive, he must see whole family! You stay!

*(CHESTER pauses, decides to stay)*

CHESTER: *(To JENNY)* This is ridiculous. I can't stay.

JENNY: I always have to. Just grin a lot when you meet this guy. Then everyone will be happy.

CHESTER: I don't wanna meet this guy!

(WILBUR *enters with* HANNAH *and* ROBERT, *who are* CHESTER'S *parents.* HANNAH *is* POPO'S *daughter. She is five years older than* JOANNE)

WILBUR: *(To* ROBERT) What? What do you mean?

AMA: *(Stands up on a chair; a speech)* Di-gou, thirty year have pass since we last see you—

WILBUR: *(To* AMA) Not now, Ma.

AMA: Do you still love God?

ROBERT: What do you mean, "What do you mean?" That's what I mean.

HANNAH: He wasn't there, Wilbur. *(To* AMA) Auntie! Di-gou isn't with us.

AMA: What? How can this be?

ROBERT: Those Chinese airliners—all junk stuffs—so inefficient.

AMA: Where is he?

POPO: *(To* ROBERT) You sure you look close?

ROBERT: What "look close"? We just waited for everyone to get off the plane.

AMA: Where is he?

HANNAH: *(To* AMA) We don't know, Auntie! *(To* CHESTER) Chester, are you packed?

AMA: Don't know?

CHESTER: *(To* HANNAH) No, I'm not. And I'm really in a hurry.

HANNAH: You're leaving tomorrow! Why aren't you packed?

CHESTER: I'm trying to, Mom.

(ROBERT *pulls out a newspaper clipping, shows it to* CHESTER)

ROBERT: Look, son, I called the Chinese paper, used a little of my influence—they did a story on you. Here—

CHESTER: *(Looks at clipping)* I can't read this, Dad! It's in Chinese.

ROBERT: *(Takes back clipping)* Little joke, there.

AMA: *(To anyone who will listen)* Where is he?

HANNAH: *(To AMA)* Auntie, ask Wilbur. *(To CHESTER)* Get packed!

CHESTER: All right!

WILBUR: *(Trying to explain to AMA)* Well, Mom, they said he wasn't at—

AMA: *(Ignoring WILBUR totally)* Where is he?

*(ROBERT continues to study the newspaper clipping, points a section out to CHESTER)*

ROBERT: Here—this is where it talks about my bank.

CHESTER: I'm going to pack.

HANNAH: *(To CHESTER)* Going?

CHESTER: *(To HANNAH)* You said I should—

HANNAH: *(To CHESTER)* You have to stay and see Di-gou!

*(WILBUR makes another attempt to explain the situation to AMA.)*

WILBUR: *(To AMA)* See, Mom, I guess—

AMA: *(Ignoring him again)* Where is he?

*(ROBERT continues studying his clipping, oblivious.)*

ROBERT: *(Translating, to CHESTER)* It says, "Great Chinese violinist will conduct and solo with New York Philharmonic."

CHESTER: What? It says what?

HANNAH: *(To Chester)* You came without being packed?

*(AMA decides to look for DI-GOU on her own, and starts searching the house.)*

AMA: Di-gou! Di-gou!

WILBUR: *(Following AMA)* Ma, listen. I'll explain.

HANNAH: *(To CHESTER)* How can you be so inefficient?

CHESTER: *(To ROBERT)* Dad, I just got a job playing in the violin section in Boston.

AMA: Di-gou! Di-gou!

CHESTER: *(To* ROBERT*)* I'm not conducting, and—

ROBERT: *(To* CHESTER*)* Ssssh! I know. but good publicity—for the bank.

HANNAH: *(To* CHESTER*)* Well, I'll help you pack later. But you have to stay till Di-gou arrives. Sheesh!

CHESTER: I can't believe this!

AMA: *(Continuing her search)* Di-gou! Are you already in bathroom? *(Exits)*

HANNAH: *(To* AMA*)* Auntie, he wasn't at the airport! *(To* WILBUR*)* Why didn't you tell her?

WILBUR: *(Following* AMA*)* I'm trying! I'm trying! *(Exits)*

ROBERT: It's those Communist airlines, I'm telling you. Inefficient.

HANNAH: We asked at the desk. They didn't have a flight list.

AMA: *(Entering)* Then where is he?

WILBUR: *(Entering, in despair)* Joanne, will you come here?

ROBERT: They probably left him in Guam.[4]

POPO: *(To* ROBERT*)* We give you that photograph. You remember to bring it?

ROBERT: Of course I remembered.

HANNAH: *(To* POPO*)* Mom, it's not Robert's fault.

POPO: *(To* HANNAH*)* Should leave him *(Refers to* ROBERT*)* in car.

HANNAH: I tried.

ROBERT: In the car?

HANNAH: He wanted to come in.

ROBERT: It's hot in the car!

AMA: *(To* ROBERT*)* Suffer, good for you.

POPO: *(To* HANNAH*)* You cannot control your husband.

ROBERT: I suffer enough.

HANNAH: He said he could help.

---

4. **Guam** (GWAHM) *n.* largest of the Mariana Islands in the West Pacific, a territory of the United States

POPO: He is wrong again.

AMA: What to do now?

(*JENNY exits in the confusion;* JOANNE *enters.*)

JOANNE: What's wrong now?

WILBUR: They lost your uncle.

JOANNE: Who lost him?

HANNAH: We didn't lose him.

AMA: *(To* ROBERT*)* You ask at airport desk?

ROBERT: I'm telling you, he's in Guam.

JOANNE: *(To* HANNAH*)* How could you lose a whole uncle?

HANNAH: We never had him to begin with!

JOANNE: So where is he?

ROBERT: Guam, I'm telling—!

POPO: *(To* ROBERT*)* Guam, Guam! Shut mouth or go there yourself!

HANNAH: *(A general announcement)* We don't know where he is!

JOANNE: Should I call the police?

WILBUR: You might have looked longer at the airport.

HANNAH: That's what I said, but he *(Refers to* ROBERT*)* said, "Aaah, too much trouble!"

POPO: *(To* ROBERT*)* See? You do not care about people from other province besides Shanghai.

ROBERT: *(To* POPO*)* Mom, I care. It's just that—

POPO: *(To* ROBERT*)* Your father trade with Japanese during war.

WILBUR: Huh?

ROBERT: Mom, let's not start that.

POPO: Not like our family. We die first!

WILBUR: What's all this about?

ROBERT: Hey, let's not bring up all this other junk, right?

POPO: *(To* ROBERT*)* You are ashamed.

ROBERT: The airport is a big place.

WILBUR: *(To* ROBERT*)* Still, you should've been able to spot an old Chinese man.

ROBERT: Everyone on that plane was an old Chinese man!

AMA: True. All Communist look alike.

HANNAH: Hold it, everybody! *(Pause)* Listen, Di-gou has this address, right?

AMA: No.

HANNAH: No? *(To* POPO*)* Mom, you said he did.

POPO: Yes. He does.

AMA: *(To* POPO*)* Yes? But I did not write to him.

POPO: I did.

AMA: Now, Communist—they will know this address.

POPO: Never mind.

AMA: No safety. Bomb us.

HANNAH: Okay, he has this address, and he can speak English—after all, he went to medical school here, right? So he shouldn't have any problem.

JOANNE: What an introduction to America.

HANNAH: All we can do is wait.

ROBERT: We went up to all these old Chinese men at the airport, asked them, "Are you our Di-gou?" They all said yes. What could we do? They all looked drunk, bums.

JOANNE: Maybe they're all still wandering through the metal detectors, looking for their families, and will continue till they die.

(CHESTER *wanders onto the tennis court, observes the following section from far upstage)*

JOANNE: I must have been only about seven the last time Di-gou visited us in the Philippines.

AMA: Less.

JOANNE: Maybee less.

WILBUR: Honey, I'm sure everyone here has a memory, too. You don't see them babbling about it, do you?

JOANNE: The last thing I remember about Di-gou, he was trying to convince you grown-ups to leave the Philippines and return to China. There was a terrible fight—one of the worst that ever took place in our complex. I guess he wanted you to join the Revolution. The fight was so loud that all our servants gathered around the windows to watch.

AMA: They did this?

POPO: Shoot them.

JOANNE: I guess this was just around 1949. Finally, Di-gou left, calling you all sorts of terrible names. On his way out, he set fire to one of our warehouses. All us kids sat around while the servants tried to put it out.

POPO: No. That was not a warehouse.

HANNAH: Yeah, Joanne—the warehouses were concrete, remember?

JOANNE: *(To HANNAH)* But don't you remember a fire?

HANNAH: Yes.

POPO: I think he burn a pile of trash.

ROBERT: *(To WILBUR)* I know how you feel. They're always yap-yap-yapping about their family stories—you'd think they were the only family in China. *(To HANNAH)* I have memories, too.

HANNAH: You don't remember anything. You have a terrible memory.

ROBERT: Look, when I was kidnapped, I didn't know—

HANNAH: Sssssh!

JOANNE: Quiet, Robert!

POPO: Like broken record—ghang, ghang, ghang.

WILBUR: *(To ROBERT)* I tell you what; you wanna take a look at my collection of tax shelters?

ROBERT: Same old stuff?

WILBUR: No. Some new ones.

*(They exit. DI-GOU appears on the tennis court; only CHESTER sees him, but CHESTER says nothing. CHESTER watches DI-GOU watching the women.)*

JOANNE: Anyway, he set fire to something and the flames burned long into the night. One servant was even killed in it, if I remember correctly. I think Matthew's nursemaid was trying to put it out when her dress caught fire and, like a fool, she ran screaming all over the complex. All the adults were too busy to hear her, I guess, and all the kids just sat there and watched this second fire, moving in circles and screaming. By morning, both fires were out, and our tutors came as usual. But that day, nothing functioned just right—I think the water pipes broke in Sah-Zip's room, the cars wouldn't start—something—all I remember is servants running around all day with one tool or another. And that was how Di-gou left Manila for the last time. Left Manila and returned to China—in two fires—one which moved—and a great rush of handymen.

*(DI-GOU is now sitting in their midst in the sunroom. He puts down his suitcase. They turn and see him. He sticks his thumb out, as if for hitch-hiking, but it is pointed in the wrong direction.)*

DI-GOU: "Going my way?"

AMA: Di-gou!

DI-GOU: "Hey, baby, got a lift?"

POPO: You see? Our family members will always return.

JOANNE: *(To DI-GOU)* Are you—? Oh, you're—? Well, nice—How did you get here?

DI-GOU: *(Pulls a book out of his jacket)* Our diplomacy handbook. Very useful.

POPO: Welcome to America!

DI-GOU: *(Referring to handbook)* It says, "When transportation is needed, put your thumb as if to plug a hole."

AMA: *(On chair)* Di-gou, thirty year have passed—

DI-GOU: *(Still reading)* "And say, 'Going my way?'"

AMA: Do you still believe in God?

DI-GOU: "Or, 'Hey, baby, got a lift?'"

AMA: Do you?

HANNAH: *(To AMA)* Auntie, he's explaining something.

DI-GOU: It worked! I am here!

AMA: *(Getting down off chair)* Still as stubborn as before.

DI-GOU: Hello, my sisters.

POPO: Hello, Di-gou. This is my daughter, Hannah.

HANNAH: *(To* DI-GOU*)* Were you at the airport? We were waiting for you.

DI-GOU: Hannah. Oh, last time, you were just a baby.

AMA: *(Introducing* JOANNE*)* And Joanne, remember?

JOANNE: Hello, Di-gou. How was your flight?

DI-GOU: Wonderful, wonderful.

POPO: Where is Chester? Chester! (CHESTER *enters the lanai)* Him—this is number one grandson.

DI-GOU: Oh, you are Chester. Your are the violinist, yes?

CHESTER: You're Di-gou?

DI-GOU: Your parents are so proud of you.

HANNAH: We are not. He's just a kid who needs to pack.

AMA: Where is Jenny? Jenny!

HANNAH: *(To* DI-GOU*)* We figured you'd be able to get here by yourself.

DI-GOU: Oh, yes.

*(He sticks out his thumb.* JENNY *enters.)*

JOANNE: Jenny! Say, "Hi, Di-gou."

JENNY: Hi, Di-gou.

DI-GOU: *(To* JOANNE*)* This is your daughter?

JOANNE: Yes. Jenny. *(Pause)* Jenny, say, "Hi, Di-gou."

JENNY: Mom, I just did!

JOANNE: Oh, Right.

JENNY: Will you cool out?

DI-GOU: Jenny, the last time I saw your mother, she was younger than you are now.

JENNY: He's kinda cute.

JOANNE: Jenny, your grand-uncle is not cute.

DI-GOU: Thank you.

JENNY: *(To* JOANNE*)* Can I go now?

AMA: Why you always want to go?

JENNY: Sorry, Ama. Busy.

JOANNE: *(Allowing* JENNY *to leave)* All right.

DI-GOU: *(To* JENNY*)* What are you doing?

JENNY: Huh? Reading
DI-GOU: Oh. Schoolwork.
JENNY: Nah. *Vogue.*[5]

   *(Exits)*

JOANNE: I've got to see about dinner. *(To* HANNAH*)* Can you give me a hand? I want to use my new Cuisinart.[6]
HANNAH: All right. What do you want to make?
JOANNE: I don't know. What does a Cuisinart do?

   *(*HANNAH *and* JOANNE *exit;* DI-GOU, AMA, POPO, *and* CHESTER *are left in the sunroom.)*

AMA: Di-gou, thirty year have pass. Do you still love God?
DI-GOU: Thirty-three.
AMA: Ah?
POPO: 1949 to 1982. Thirty-three. He is correct.
AMA: Oh. But you do still love God? Like before?
DI-GOU: You know, sisters, after you left China, I learned that I never did believe in God.

   *(Pause)*

AMA: What!
POPO: How can you say this?
CHESTER: Ama, Popo, don't start in on that—he just got here.
POPO: You defend him?
AMA: *(Chasing* CHESTER *out to tennis court)* You both are influence by bad people.
POPO: Spend time with bums! Communist bum, musician bum, both same.
DI-GOU: Just to hear my sisters after all these years—you may speak whatever you like.
AMA: Do you still love God?

---

5. **Vogue** (VOHG) *n.* the name of a fashion magazine
6. **Cuisinart** (KWEE-zuhn-ahrt) *n.* a machine that chops food

DI-GOU: I have much love.

AMA: For God?

DI-GOU: For my sisters.

*(Pause)*

POPO: You are being very difficult.

AMA: You remember when you first become Christian?

POPO: You travel with See-goh-poh on her first evangelism tour? Before we move to Philippines and you stay in China? Remember? You speak in tongues of fire.

DI-GOU: I was only eight years old. That evening is a blur to me.

AMA: Tonight—we have family devotions. You can speak again. Miracles. You still believe in miracles?

DI-GOU: It is a miracle that I am here again with you!

POPO: Why you always change subject? You remember Ah Hong? Your servant? How See-goh-poh cast out his opium demon?

DI-GOU: I don't think that happened.

AMA: Yes! Remember? After evangelism tour—she cast out his demon.

POPO: Ah Hong tell stories how he . . . can see everything so clear, like—uh—glass. He can see even through wall, he say, and can see—ah—all the way through floor. Yes! . . . And he talk with Satan and demon who pretend to be Ah Hong's dead uncles. You should remember.

DI-GOU: I vaguely recall some such stories.

*(DI-GOU opens up his suitcase during POPO's following speech and takes out two small Chinese toys and a small Chinese flag. He shows them to POPO, but she tries to ignore them.)*

POPO: Demon pretend to be ghost, then show himself everyplace to Ah Hong—in kitchen, in well, in barn, in street of village. Always just sit there, never talk, never move, just sit. So See-goh-poh come, call on God, say only, "Demon begone."

AMA: And from then on, no more ghost, no more opium.

POPO: You—you so happy, then. You say, you will also cast out the demon.

DI-GOU: We were all just children.

*(He lines the toys up on the floor.)*

AMA: But you have faith of a child.

DI-GOU: Ah Hong didn't stop eating opium, though. He just needed money. That's why two years later, he was fired!

POPO: I don't think so.

DI-GOU: Yes, my tenth, eleventh birthday, he was fired.

AMA: No—remember? Ah Hong die many year later—just before you come to America for college.

DI-GOU: No, he was fired before then.

POPO: No. Before you leave, go to college, you must prepare your own suitcase. *(To AMA)* Bad memory.

AMA: Brainwash.

*(ROBERT and WILBUR enter; CHESTER exits off the tennis court. ROBERT and WILBUR surround DI-GOU.)*

ROBERT and WILBUR: Welcome!

WILBUR: How you doing, Di-gow?

ROBERT: *(Correcting WILBUR)* Di-gou!

WILBUR: Oh, right. "Di-gou."

ROBERT: *(To DI-GOU)* We tried to find you at the airport.

WILBUR: *(To DI-GOU)* That means "second brother."

ROBERT: So, you escaped the Communists, huh?

WILBUR: Robert and I were just—

ROBERT: Little joke, there.

WILBUR: —looking at my collection of tax shelters.

ROBERT: China's pretty different now, huh?

WILBUR: You care to take a look?

ROBERT: I guess there's never a dull moment—

WILBUR: Probably no tax shelters, either.

ROBERT: —waiting for the next cultural revolution.

WILBUR: Oh, Robert!

ROBERT: Little joke, there.

WILBUR: *(To* DI-GOU*)* That's how he *(Refers to* ROBERT*)* does business.

ROBERT: Of course, I respect China.

WILBUR: He says these totally outrageous things.

ROBERT: But your airlines—so inefficient.

WILBUR: And people remember him?

ROBERT: How long were you in Guam?

WILBUR: *(To* ROBERT*)* He wasn't in Guam!

ROBERT: No?

WILBUR: *(To* DI-GOU*)* Well, we're going to finish up the tour.

ROBERT: My shelters are all at my house.

WILBUR: Feel welcome to come along.

ROBERT: His *(Refers to* WILBUR*)* are kid stuff. Who wants land in Montana?

WILBUR: *(To* ROBERT*)* Hey—I told you. I need the loss.

(WILBUR *and* ROBERT *exit, leaving* DI-GOU *with* AMA *and* POPO. *There is a long silence.)*

DI-GOU: Who are they?

POPO: Servants.

AMA: Don't worry. They will eat outside. In America, servants do not take over their masters' house.

DI-GOU: What are you talking about?

AMA: We know. In China now, servants beat their masters.

DI-GOU: Don't be ridiculous. I have a servant. A chauffeur.

(ROBERT *reenters)*

ROBERT: Hey, Di-gou—we didn't even introduce ourselves.

DI-GOU: Oh, my sisters explained it to me.

ROBERT: I'm Robert. Hannah's my wife. (ROBERT *puts his arm around* DI-GOU.) When we married, I had nothing. I was working in grocery stores, fired from one job after another. But she could tell—I had a good heart.

DI-GOU: It is good to see servants marrying into the

moneyed ranks. We are not aware of such progress by even the lowest classes.

*(Pause)*

ROBERT: Huh?

DI-GOU: To come to this—from the absolute bottom of society.

ROBERT: Wait, wait. I mean, sure, I made progress, but "the bottom of society"? That's stretching it some, wouldn't you say?

DI-GOU: Did you meet Hannah while preparing her food?

ROBERT: Huh? No, we met at a foreign students' dance at UCLA.

DI-GOU: Oh. You attended university?

ROBERT: Look, I'm not a country kid. It's not like I was that poor. I'm from Shanghai, you know.

POPO: *(To ROBERT)* Ssssh! Neighbors will hear!

ROBERT: I'm cosmopolitan. So when I went to college I just played around at first. That's the beauty of the free-enterprise system, Di-gou. If you wanna be a bum, it lets you be a bum. I wasted my time, went out with all those American girls.

POPO: One girl.

ROBERT: Well, one was more serious, a longer commitment . . .

POPO: Minor.

DI-GOU: What?

POPO: He go out with girl—only fifteen year old.

ROBERT: I didn't know!

POPO: *(To ROBERT)* How come you cannot ask?

ROBERT: I was just an FOB.[7] This American girl—she talked to me—asked me out—kissed me on first date—and I thought, "Land of opportunity!" Anyway, I decided to turn my back on China.

---

7. **FOB** fresh off the boat, an expression used about recent immigrants

POPO: *(To* DI-GOU*)* He cannot even ask girl how old.

ROBERT: This is my home. When I wanted to stop being a bum, make money, it let me. That's America.

DI-GOU: I also attended American university. Columbia Medical School.

ROBERT: Right. My wife told me.

POPO: *(To* ROBERT*)* But he does not date the minor!

ROBERT: *(To* POPO*)* How was I supposed to know? She looked fully developed!

(AMA *and* POPO *leave in disgust, leaving* ROBERT *alone with* DI-GOU.*)*

ROBERT: *(To* DI-GOU*)* Well, then, you must understand American ways.

DI-GOU: It has been some time since I was in America.

ROBERT: Well, it's improved a lot, lemme tell you. Look, I have a friend who's an immigration lawyer. If you want to stay here, he can arrange it.

DI-GOU: Oh, no. The thought never even—

ROBERT: I know, but listen. I did it. Never had any regrets. We might be able to get your family over, too.

DI-GOU: Robert, I cannot leave China.

ROBERT: Huh? Look, Di-gou, people risk their lives to come to America. If only you could talk to—to the boat people.

DI-GOU: Uh—the food here looks very nice.

ROBERT: Huh? Oh, help yourself, Go ahead.

DI-GOU: Thank you. I will wait.

ROBERT: No, go on!

DI-GOU: Thank you, but—

ROBERT: Look, in America, there's so much, we don't have to be polite at all!

DI-GOU: Please—I'm not yet hungry.

ROBERT: Us Chinese, we love to eat, right? Well, here in America, we can be pigs!

DI-GOU: I'm not hungry.

ROBERT: I don't see why you can't—? Look. *(He picks up a piece of food, a* bao.*)* See? *(He stuffs the whole thing into his mouth.)* Pigs!

DI-GOU: Do you mind? I told you, I'm not—

ROBERT: I know. You're not hungry. Think I'm hungry? No, sir! What do I have to do to convince you? Here. *(He drops a tray of* guo-tieh *on the ground, begins stomping them.)* This is the land of plenty!

DI-GOU: Ai! Robert!

*(ROBERT continues stomping them like roaches.)*

ROBERT: There's one next to your foot! *(He stomps it.)* Gotcha!

DI-GOU: Please! It is not right to step on food!

ROBERT: "Right?" Now, see, that's your problem in the P.R.C.[8]—lots of justice, but you don't produce.

*(WILBUR enters, catching ROBERT in the act.)*

WILBUR: Robert? What are you—? What's all this?

ROBERT: *(Stops stamping)* What's the big deal? You got a cleaning woman, don't you?

*(JENNY enters.)*

JENNY: Time to eat yet? *(She sees the mess.)* Blaagh.

*(HANNAH enters.)*

HANNAH: What's all this?

JENNY: Never mind.

*(JENNY exits; WILBUR points to ROBERT, indicating to HANNAH that ROBERT is responsible for the mess. AMA and POPO also enter at this moment, and see WILBUR'S indication.)*

DI-GOU: In China, the psychological problems of wealth are a great concern.

POPO: Ai! Who can clean up after man like this!

WILBUR: Robert, I just don't think this is proper.

AMA: Wilbur—not clean himself.

---

8. **P.R.C.** abbreviation for the People's Republic of China

ROBERT: Quiet! You all make a big deal out of nothing!

DI-GOU: I am a doctor. I understand.

POPO: But Robert—he also has the fungus feet.

ROBERT: Shut up, everybody! Will you all just shut up? I was showing Di-gou American ways!

(WILBUR *takes* DI-GOU's *arm.*)

WILBUR: *(To* DI-GOU*)* Uh—come out here. I'll show you some American ways.

(WILBUR *and* DI-GOU *go out to the tennis court.*)

ROBERT: *(To* WILBUR*)* What do you know about American ways? You were born here!

POPO: *(To* AMA*)* Exercise—good for him.

ROBERT: Only us immigrants really know American ways!

POPO: *(To* AMA, *pinching her belly)* Good for here.

HANNAH: *(To* ROBERT*)* Shut up, dear. You've done enough damage today.

(WILBUR *gets* DI-GOU *a racket.*)

AMA: *(To* POPO*)* In China, he *(Refers to* DI-GOU*)* receives plenty of exercise. Whenever Communists, they come torture him.

WILBUR: *(On tennis court, to* DI-GOU*)* I'll set up the machine. *(He goes* OFF.*)*

ROBERT: *(In sunroom, looking at tennis court)* What's so American about tennis?

HANNAH: *(To* ROBERT*)* Yes, dear.

ROBERT: You all ruined it!

HANNAH: You ruined the *guo-tieh,* dear.

ROBERT: What's a few *guo-tieh* in defense of America?

DI-GOU: *(To* WILBUR*)* I have not played tennis since my college days at Columbia.

ROBERT: *(To* HANNAH*)* He *(refers to* DI-GOU*)* was being so cheap! Like this was a poor country!

HANNAH: He's lived in America before, dear.

ROBERT: That was years ago. When we couldn't even buy a house in a place like this.

HANNAH: We still can't.

ROBERT: What?

HANNAH: Let's face it. We still can't afford—

ROBERT: That's not what I mean, stupid! I mean, when we wouldn't be able to because we're Chinese. He doesn't know the new America. I was making a point and you all ruined it!

HANNAH: Yes, dear. Now let's go in and watch the Betamax.

ROBERT: No!

HANNAH: C'mon! (ROBERT and HANNAH exit)

(On the tennis court, DI-GOU and WILBUR stand next to each other, facing offstage. A machine offstage begins to shoot tennis balls at them, each ball accompanied by a small explosive sound. A ball goes by; DI-GOU tries to hit it, but it is too high for him. Two more balls go by, but they are also out of DI-GOU's reach. A fourth ball is shot out, which hits WILBUR.)

WILBUR: Aaaah!

(Balls are being shot out much faster now, pummeling WILBUR and DI-GOU. AMA and POPO continue to sit in the sunroom, staring away from the tennis court, peaceful and oblivious.)

DI-GOU: Aaah!

WILBUR: I don't—! This never happened—!

DI-GOU: Watch out!

WILBUR: I'll turn off the machine.

DI-GOU: Good luck! Persevere! Overcome! Oh! Watch—!

(A volley of balls drives WILBUR back. AMA and POPO hear the commotion, look over to the tennis court. The balls stop shooting out.)

ROBERT: Tennis.

AMA: A fancy machine.

(They return to looking downstage. The balls begin again.)

WILBUR: Oh, no!

AMA: Wilbur—he is such a bad loser.

POPO: Good exercise, huh? His age—good for here.

*(She pinches her belly.)*

DI-GOU: I will persevere!

*(DI-GOU tries to get to the machine, is driven back)*

WILBUR: No! Di-gow!
DI-GOU: I am overcome!
WILBUR: Joanne!

*(He begins crawling like a guerrilla toward the machine and finally makes it offstage. The balls stop, presumably because WILBUR reached the machine. DI-GOU runs off the court.)*

DI-GOU: (Breathless) Is it time yet . . . that we may cease to have . . . such enjoyment?

*(WILBUR crosses back onto the tennis court and into the lanai.)*

WILBUR: (To offstage) JOANNE! This machine's too fast. I don't pay good money to be attacked by my possessions! *(Exits)*

*(AMA and POPO get up, exit into the house, applauding DI-GOU as they go, for his exercise.)*

AMA and POPO: (Clapping) Good, good, very good!

*(DI-GOU is left alone on the tennis court. He is hit by a lone tennis ball. CHESTER enters, with a violin case. It is obvious that he has thrown that ball.)*

CHESTER: Quite a workout, there.
DI-GOU: America is full of surprises—why do all these products function so poorly?
CHESTER: Looks like "Made in U.S." is gonna become synonymous with defective workmanship. *(Pause)* You wanna see my violin?
DI-GOU: I would love to.
CHESTER: I thought you might. Here.

*(He removes the violin from its case.)*

CHESTER: See? No "Made in U.S." label.

DI-GOU: It is beautiful.

CHESTER: Careful! The back has a lacquer which never dries—so don't touch it, or you'll leave fingerprints in it forever.

DI-GOU: Imagine that. After I die, someone could be playing a violin with my fingerprint.

CHESTER: Funny, isn't it?

DI-GOU: Though I never had as fine an instrument as this.

CHESTER: Try it. Go ahead.

DI-GOU: No. Please. I get more pleasure looking at it than I would playing it. But I would get the most pleasure hearing you play.

CHESTER: No.

DI-GOU: Please?

CHESTER: All right. Later. How long did you play?

DI-GOU: Some years. During the Cultural Revolution, I put it down.

CHESTER: Must've been tough, huh? (CHESTER *directs* DI-GOU's *attention to the back of his violin.*) Look—the back's my favorite part.

DI-GOU: China is my home, my work. I had to stay there.

(DI-GOU *looks at the back of the violin.*) Oh—the way the light reflects—look. And I can see myself in it.

CHESTER: Yeah. Nice, huh?

DI-GOU: So you will take this violin and make music around the world.

CHESTER: Around the world? Oh, you probably got a misleading press clipping. See, my dad . . .

DI-GOU: Very funny.

CHESTER: (*Smiling*) Yeah. See, I'm just playing in the Boston Symphony. I'm leaving tomorrow.

DI-GOU: I am fortunate, then, to come today, or perhaps I would never meet you.

CHESTER: You know, I wasn't even planning to come here.

DI-GOU: That would be terrible. You know, in China, my wife and I had no children—for the good of the state.

(*DI-GOU moves to where he left the Chinese toys earlier in the act. He picks them up and studies them.*)

DI-GOU: All these years, I try to imagine—what does Hannah look like: What does her baby look like? Now, I finally visit and what do I find? A young man. A violinist. The baby has long since disappeared. And I learn I'll never know the answer to my question.

(*Silence*)

CHESTER: Di-gou, why did you come here?

DI-GOU: My wife has died, I'm old. I've come for my sisters.

CHESTER: Well, I hope you're not disappointed to come here and see your sisters, your family, carry on like this.

DI-GOU: They are still my sisters.

CHESTER: I'm leaving here. Like you did.

DI-GOU: But, Chester, I've found that I cannot leave the family. Today—look! I follow them across an ocean.

CHESTER: You know, they're gonna start bringing you to church.

DI-GOU: No. My sisters and their religion are two different things.

CHESTER: No, they're not. You've been away. You've forgotten. This family breathes for God. Ever since your aunt, See-goh-poh.

DI-GOU: See-goh-poh is not the first member of this family.

CHESTER: She's the first Christian.

DI-GOU: There are faces back further than you can see. Faces long before the white missionaries arrived in China. Here. (*He holds* CHESTER's *violin so that its back is facing* CHESTER, *and uses it like a mirror.*) Look here. At your face. Study your face and you will see—the shape of your face is the shape of the faces back many generations—

across an ocean, in another soil. You must become one
with your family before you can hope to live away from it.

CHESTER: Oh, sure, there're faces. But they don't matter
here. See-goh-poh's face is the only one that has any
meaning here.

DI-GOU: No. The stories written on your face are the ones
you must believe.

CHESTER: Stories? I see stories, Di-gou. All around me.
This house tells a story. The days of the week tell a
story—Sunday is service, Wednesday and Friday are
fellowship, Thursday is visitation. Even the furniture tells
stories. Look around. See-goh-poh is sitting in every
chair. There's nothing for me here.

DI-GOU: I am here.

CHESTER: You? All right. Here. (CHESTER *turns the back
of the violin around toward* DI-GOU, *again using it like a
mirror.*) You look. You wanna know what I see? I see the
shape of your face changing. And with it, a mind, a will,
as different as the face. If you stay with them, your old
self will go, and in its place will come a new man, an old
man, a man who'll pray.

DI-GOU: Chester, you are in America. If you deny those
who share your blood, what do you have in this country?

AMA: *(From offstage)* All right? Ready?

CHESTER: Your face is changing, Di-gou. Before you know
it, you'll be praying and speaking in tongues.

AMA: *(Still offstage)* One, two, three, four!

(*The "Hallelujah Chorus" begins. The choir enters, consisting
of* WILBUR, JOANNE, ROBERT, HANNAH *and* POPO.
*They're led by* AMA, *who stands at a movable podium which is
being pushed into the room by* ROBERT *and* WILBUR *as they
sing. The choir heads for the center of the room, where the
podium comes to rest, with* AMA *still on it, and the
"Hallelujah Chorus" ends.* ROBERT *begins singing the tenor
aria "Every Valley Shall Be Exalted," from Handel's* Messiah.)

ROBERT: "Every valley, every valley . . ."

HANNAH: Quiet, Robert!

ROBERT: But I want my solo!

JOANNE: *(To* ROBERT*)* Sssh! We already decided this.

ROBERT: *(Continuing to sing)* ". . . shall be exalted . . ."

JOANNE: *(Yelling offstage)* Jenny!

AMA: *(To* ROBERT*)* Time for Family Devotions! Set up room!

> *(They begin to arrange the room like a congregation hall, with the pulpit up front.)*

ROBERT: But it's a change to hear my beautiful voice.

JENNY: *(From offstage)* Yeah! What?

POPO: *(To* ROBERT*)* Hear at home, hear in car. Now set up room.

JOANNE: *(Yelling offstage)* Jenny, Devotions!

JENNY: *(From offstage)* Aw, Mom.

JOANNE: *(Yelling offstage)* Devotions!

JENNY: *(Entering)* All right.

ROBERT: *(To* HANNAH*)* You know what this is? This is the breakdown of family authority.

HANNAH: *(To* ROBERT*)* You have all the authority, dear. Now shut up.

> *(*JENNY *goes over to* CHESTER.*)*

JENNY: Hey, you still here? I thought for sure you'd have split by now.

CHESTER: I will.

JENNY: You gotta take it easier. Do like me. I act all lotus blossom for them. I say, "Hi, uncle this and auntie that." It's easy.

ROBERT: Look—all this free time. *(Sings)* "Every valley . . ."

POPO: Shoot him!

(The room is set up.)

AMA: We begin! Family Devotions!

> *(*AMA *flips a switch. A neon cross is lit up.)*

JENNY: *(To* CHESTER*)* Looks like a disco.

*(Everyone is seated except DI-GOU. The rest of the family waits for him. He walks over and sits down. AMA bows down to pray. Everyone bows except CHESTER and DI-GOU, but since all other eyes are closed, no one notices their noncompliance. AMA begins to pray.)*

AMA: Dear Father, when we think of your great mercy to this family, we can only feel so grateful, privilege to be family chose for your work. You claim us to be yours, put your mark on our heart.

*(CHESTER gets up, picks up his violin, gets DI-GOU's attention.)*

AMA: Your blessing begin many year ago in China.

*(CHESTER begins playing; his music serves as underscoring to AMA's prayer.)*

AMA: When See-goh-poh, she hear your word—from missionary. Your spirit, it touch her heart, she accept you, she speak in tongue of fire.

*(CHESTER begins to move out of the room as he plays.)*

AMA: You continue, bless See-goh-poh. She become agent of God, bring light to whole family, until we are convert, we become shining light for you all through Amoy.

*(CHESTER stops playing, looks at DI-GOU, waves good-bye, and exits. DI-GOU gets up, walks to where CHESTER was standing before he left, and waves good-bye.)*

AMA: Let us praise your victory over Satan. Praise your power over demon. Praise miracle over our own sinful will. Praise your victory over even our very hearts. Amen.

*(AMA conducts the choir in the ending of the "Hallelujah Chorus." As they sing, she notices DI-GOU's chair is empty. She turns and sees him waving. They look at each other as the "Hallelujah Chorus" continues.)*

END OF ACT ONE

# AFTER YOU READ

## Exchanging Backgrounds and Cultures

1. What does the mispronunciation of Di-Gou's name by Jenny and Chester reveal about their attitude toward their heritage?

2. Why do you think Robert throws the food on the floor? What does this act suggest about his values? What does this suggest about Robert's interpretation of American values?

3. What does the phrase "family devotions" mean to Ama and Popo? How does their idea of family devotion differ from Di-Gou's?

## What Do You Think?

Which character or situation in this act was most meaningful to you? Why?

## Experiencing Drama

The first act of *Family Devotions* ends with the departure of Chester, while Ama and Popo lead the family in religious prayer. What do you think might happen next? Jot your ideas down on a piece of paper. Then write a brief second act in which you resolve the action of the drama.

*Optional Activity* Write a short play about a gathering or reunion of your own family or friends. Remember to use stage directions that describe the setting, as well as dialogue that reveals the personalities and relationships of the characters.

# UNIT 4: FOCUS ON WRITING

Dramas are generally meant to be performed not read. As a result, when you write a drama, you must work within the limitations of a performance.

## Writing a Dramatic Sketch

A dramatic sketch is a shortened form of drama, consisting of one brief scene that makes a single point. Like longer forms of drama, a dramatic sketch will also include dialogue and stage directions. Write a dramatic sketch about a personal milestone, a memorable experience shared with your friends or family, or another topic of your choice.

## The Writing Process

Good writing requires both time and effort. An effective writer completes a number of stages that together make up the writing process. The stages of the writing process are given below to help guide you through your assignment.

### Prewriting

If you have difficulty coming up with a topic, you may want to try using group storytelling or a self-interview to collect writing ideas. To hold a group storytelling session, gather with two or three of your classmates, and share real and imaginary stories. One of your own stories or one told by a classmate may spark an idea for your dramatic sketch.

Once you have decided on a topic, outline the plot, or sequence of events, of your sketch. How will it begin? How will the central conflict be introduced and resolved? How will it end? Remember that you must choose events that can be presented on stage. Avoid events and situations that will be difficult to reproduce or will require a great amount of space.

Next, decide on a group of characters and make a list of their names. Next to each name, write a brief description of that character. How will the characters look? How will they act? How will they talk?

Finally, consider the setting of your sketch. Make a list of the movable objects, or props, you will need. Remember that the props and costumes should reflect the time period in which the action occurs.

### Drafting and Revising

Now you are ready to begin drafting. Start your sketch by listing the characters. Following this list, write a set of stage directions that includes a detailed description of the setting.

Next, write the dialogue and the stage directions that describe the action of the sketch. The dialogue should reveal the personalities of your characters. For instance, in *Family Devotions,* Jenny and Chester's conversations and figures of speech show that they are modern-day American teenagers. Remember that even the most basic information, such as the characters' names, must be conveyed through the dialogue.

After you have finished drafting, revise your work. Remember that a dramatic sketch should be brief and make a single point. Therefore, the dialogue and stage directions should directly relate to the purpose of the sketch. Cut excessive and unrelated information. Make sure that the dialogue sounds like realistic and natural conversation.

### Proofreading and Publishing

Proofread the sketch, correcting any errors in spelling, grammar, punctuation, and capitalization. Then make a neat final copy.

Now your scene is ready to be performed! Choose actors from among your classmates and perform the play for other classes in your school.

154

## LITERATURE ACKNOWLEDGMENTS

Globe Book Company wishes to thank the following copyright owners for permission to reproduce literature in this book.

BOA Editions Ltd., 92 Park Avenue, Brockport, NY 14420: Li-Young Lee, "Eating Together" from *Rose.* Copyright © 1986 by Li-Young Lee.

Diana Chang: Diana Chang, "Saying Yes" from *American-Asian Anthology.* Copyright © by Diana Chang.

Ling Chung: Ling Chung, "A Soil With Rain and Sunshine" from *Asian-American Heritage: An Anthology of Prose and Poetry,* ed. David Hsin-Fu Wand. Copyright © 1974 by Ling Chung.

Sandra Kijkstra Literary Agency for Amy Tan: Amy Tan, "My Mother's English" from *Threepenny Review.* Copyright © 1990 by Amy Tan.

HarperCollins Publishers: Laurence Yep, "The Land of the Demons" from *Dragonwings.* Copyright © 1975 by Laurence Yep.

Pardee Lowe, Sr.: Pardee Lowe, Sr., excerpt from *Father and Glorious Descendant.* Copyright © 1937, 1938, 1941, 1943 by Pardee Lowe.

Lum, Wing Tek: Wing Tek Lum, "Minority Poem." from *Asian-American Heritage: An Anthology of Prose and Poetry,* ed. David Hsin-Fu Wand. Copyright © 1974 Wing Tek Lum.

Laureen Mar: Laureen Mar, "Chinatown #1" from *The Greenfield Review* vol. 6 nos. 1 & 2 (spring 1977), guest edited by Garrett Kaoru Hongo. Copyright © 1977 by Laureen Mar.

Diana Ming Chan: Monfoon Leong, "Number One Son." Copyright © 1975 by Diana Ming Chan, Library of Congress, catalog card number 74-84460.

Lensey Namioka and Ruth Cohen, Agent: Lensey Namioka, "The All-American Slurp" from *Visions,* ed. Donald R. Gallo.

New American Library: David Henry Hwang, excerpt from Act One of *Family Devotions* from *FOB and Other Plays.* Copyright © David Henry Hwang.

University of Washington Press: Jade Snow Wong, excerpt from Chapter 5 of *Fifth Chinese Daughter.* Copyright © 1945, 1948, 1950 by Jade Snow Wong.

Elizabeth Wong: Elizabeth Wong, "The Struggle to Be an All-American Girl," *Los Angeles Times,* September 7, 1980. Copyright © 1980 Elizabeth Wong.

Yale University Press: Cathy Song, "Lost Sister" from *Picture Bride.* Copyright © 1983 by Cathy Song.

Globe Book Company has executed a reasonable and concerted effort to contact the authors of the following poems: "a chinese landscape painting in california—18?," by Alan Ching Lau, and "Grandfather," by James Lim. Globe Book Company eagerly invites any persons knowledgable about the whereabouts of these authors or agents to contact Globe Book Company to arrange for the customary publishing transactions.

## ART AND PHOTO ACKNOWLEDGMENTS

*cover*  Untitled, 1984, Pamela Chin Lee, courtesy of the *Asian American Arts Center*

**p. 3**  San Francisco, Chinatown, Craig Aurness/Woodfin Camp and Associates

**p. 27**  **My Secret World,** Martin Wong, courtesy of the *Asian American Arts Center*

**p. 93**  Untitled, Pamela Chin Lee, courtesy of the *Asian American Arts Center*

**p. 111**  **In Front of Christmas Blossoms,** Tsai-Tung Chang, *Hanart Gallery,* Hong Kong